SOMAN GOUDA
(ANIKETANA)

YOGI IN SUITS
CHRISTOPHER NOLAN AND VEDANTA

SOMAN GOUDA
(ANIKETANA)

YOGI IN SUITS
CHRISTOPHER NOLAN AND VEDANTA

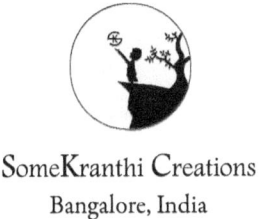

SomeKranthi Creations
Bangalore, India

SomeKranthi Creations
India

Published by SomeKranthi Creations
16/2, 3rd Floor, Muniswamappa Road, Halasuru,
Bangalore 560008, Karnataka, India
Mob: 9985007590
somekranthi@gmail.com

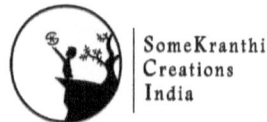

Copyright © Soman Gouda
First Print : 2018
Pages : xviii + 166 = 184
Used Paper : 70 GSM Book Print
Book Size : Demy 1/8th

All rights reserved

The views and opinions expressed in this are the author's own and are as reported by him which have been verified to extent possible, and the publishers are not in any way liable for the same.

Typeset in Adobe Garamond Premr Pro by Lakshmi Mudranalaya, Bangalore

This book is sold subject to the conditon that it shall not, by way of trade or otherwise, be lent, resold, hired out, or otherwise circulated without the publisher's prior consent in any form of binding or cover other than that in which it is published and without a similar condition including this condition being imposed on the subsequent purchaser.

A leap of faith from Batman to Brahman!

After the years of solitary labor, they wrote the great accounts called Upanishads, without even writing their own names on them. I bow down to those 'unknowns' who really 'knew', and dedicate this book to their will.

To those who have kept the art alive, by resonating the souls through their masterpieces. I bow down to all the artists of the world and dedicate this book to them.

CONTENTS

Introduction

    I. Why this book?   ix
    II. Why I wrote this book?   xi
    III. Why should you read this book?   xvi

Chapter 1   Why the world cannot ignore Nolan?   01

Chapter 2   Doodlebug to Dunkirk   17

Chapter 3   Vedanta and Nolan Cinema   33

Chapter 4   Law of feelings and emotions   61

Chapter 5   Einstein + Kurosawa   77

Chapter 6   When I interviewed Christopher Nolan   95

Chapter 7   Yogi in Suits   105

Chapter 8   Art: The universal religion   120

Chapter 9   Chase your reality   137

Chapter 10   Random thoughts of an unaccomplished mind   153

Om poornamadah poornamidam poornaat poornamudachyate
Poornasya poornamaadaaya poornamevaavashishyate
Om shaantih shaantih shaantih ||

"That (Brahman) is complete, and this (universe) is complete.
The complete proceeds from the complete.
(Then) Taking the completeness from the complete (universe),
it remains as the complete (Brahman) alone."
Om peace peace peace ||

-Ishavasya Upanishad

INTRODUCTION

Why this book?

I believe, it is no less than a sin to die without making an attempt, to know what we came here for, that is, 'the reality' or 'the truth of existence'. Right from the times of Vedas, it is the quest of man and still remains an unsolved puzzle. People from eastern part of the world, sat in dark caves and explored the inner world through the days and nights to find out what it is. Whereas, the western part of the world settled in sophisticated laboratories, built telescopes and kissed the surface of the moon. Latter can be witnessed but former cannot be. In other words, east tried to find out the nature of universe in the psychic sphere, while the west attempted to discover the basic building block of the universe. It was all a game of mind and matter.

For many centuries, most of the scientists have managed to shun the door of metaphysics. It's because they are scientists! They don't want to mix up (mess up?) with philosophy. They say, 'I can show you the bulb and telephone that I invented, can you show me your truth or some enlightenment?' This attitude of division between the science and philosophy takes us nowhere. People like Nikola Tesla and Albert Einstein outshined rest of the flock, since they embraced both of them. Greek sages like Socrates, Plato, Aristotle and Pythagoras were all polymaths and made efforts through both scientific and philosophical approaches. These sages proved that the science and philosophy corroborate each other, when we go deeper into them. These two were not separate streams in the beginning, as everything originated from the same mind. Now, it is great to see that there is a significant research taking place to understand the consciousness consciously. In cosmology, we have reached to an extent where we know what is there millions of light years away and can estimate the size of a black hole, which is 1 million times bigger than our home planet-earth. And we are able to speculate on the nature and building blocks of it, which was thought to be inconceivable and unfathomable. It's no surprise if our children go on a space vacation in the near future.

When we observe the history of mankind closely, we notice a fact and pattern that man always tried to express his experiences. The process of exploration and expression went together hand in hand, and that is how the art came into picture. Art is created out of insights and so it provides insights to the audience. "What comes from the heart goes to the heart" said Coleridge. Like the river taking different courses, art found its different forms from Literature to Sculpture, Painting to Music and they reached their pinnacle during the renaissance period. After the industrial revolution in the 19th century, when the west started embracing the luxurious life, many scientific inventions were made. It led to a proliferation of a new art form called cinema or motion pictures. Gradually it evolved from black and white silent films to a new IMAX and 3D films. Cinema became an inevitable part of our lives. Films progressed to a magnitude where they dominate over all other art forms and influence the very culture and lifestyle of the people. Cinema is woven into the very fabric of modern society.

Assume when you explore the truth from all three of artistic, scientific and philosophical approaches, you find new visions and then you deliver them to the world in a most beautiful and comprehensible manner. It's just like you are taking all the people through your own subjective psychic journey. How would it be?

Christopher Nolan, a British-American film director is making such a noble and honest effort. The splendor here is, he takes along the whole generation as part of his endeavor. It's because he does it through a globally shared medium called cinema. His intellectual curiosity, poetic consciousness and ingenious filmmaking style make him a perfect fusion of art, science and philosophy. Nolan seems like a combination of Akira Kurosawa and Albert Einstein, yet as innocent as, a bewildered kid in front of a grand toy house with the name Universe. I would say "If you don't believe in Christ, believe in Chris".

Vedanta is both science and art, science because it is the result of experiments and experiences of yogis, and art because it is a method and a way of life. Christopher Nolan himself is an artist and a scientist, so he must be a Yogi. This title is not an effort to idolize a person but to appreciate and admire the thoughts. This book is an attempt to shed the light on an obscured commune between the east and the west; past and the future; black hole and the soul..

Why I wrote this book?

I had never thought that I would write a book like this in my life. An idea! 'resilient and highly contagious' was formed a few years ago, when the film 'Inception' was released. But the genesis of the thought dates back to my childhood. When I was in high school, my teacher told me that, there are 10^{23} stars in the universe and many stars born and die every day. Most of them are bigger than our Sun. The universe is still expanding; there are millions of stars in a galaxy and millions of such galaxies in the universe. I was enthralled! The very next moment I felt a little disturbed. Reason for my disconcerted state was the question, 'In this vast universe, where is the significance of earth and myself?' But then I began thinking and came to an optimistic conclusion that man is great. Only he could count these stars and knows that the universe is so huge and unbound! No other creatures. That stream of thought continued and led me to question the level-headedness of traversing the universe. Is it really sensible and practical to explore this? We are still struggling to reconnoiter our neighbor Mars and unable to cross the solar system. I get merely 70 to 80 years of life on this planet, should I waste it in studying them? Even if I join NASA, I can only know the surface of our vicinal planets in this life, I felt. As I grew up, I realized that it is very essential for the evolution of man.

However my quest continued, where this all creation emanated from? This vast matter! Who created it? Is it not enough to know this universe? What if there are many such universes? How to know about its creation? Who witnessed its beginning? I just wanted to know it before I die! And also wanted to know where I will go if I die. I was not too serious (vyakulata) about it but it was there in a corner of my mind always. Then I came across following lines of Swami Vivekananda in a book (Jnana Yoga) which was gifted to me by my brother. "'If I know one lump of clay, I know the whole mass of clay.' The universe is all built on the same plan. The individual is only a part, like the lump of clay. If we know the human soul—which is one atom—its beginning and general history, we know the whole of nature. Birth, growth, development, decay, death—this is the sequence in all nature and is the same in the plant and the man. The difference is only in time. The whole cycle may be completed in one case in a day, in the other in three score years and ten; the methods are the same. The only way to reach a sure analysis of the universe is by the analysis of our own minds."

I was the happiest person in the universe then. How true! I uttered within myself. Then my journey in the spiritual world commenced. I surrendered to the creator of this universe; started reading, watching and listening to the discourses of all great souls. From Buddha, Mahavira, Shankara to Basava, Ramakrishna to the recent rebels like Ramana Maharshi, Osho, J Krishnamurthy, and Allan Watts and so on. In this expedition, I was very fortunate to be exposed to most of the great saints and philosophers from both the east and the west, who left their footprints on sands of time. I thought, I should have lived in the times of Buddha or Shankara or Rama Krishna, nevertheless I felt blessed when I saw his holiness Shri Siddheshwara Swamiji of Jnana Yogashrama Bijapur, India. We heard Buddha enlightened ten thousand men along with him and he imparted wisdom all his life; Shankara at his very young age wrote commentaries (Bhashyas) on Prasthanathrayi (Upanishads, Brahmasutras and Gita) with an unparalleled wisdom and sagacity, revered as a Jagadguru(Guru of the Universe) by the entire India; Ramakrishna was an embodiment of Bhakti (devotion), who simplified very complex spiritual thoughts and sandwiched sublime vedantic knowledge in his fables and jokes to teach a common man effectively, he was a saint, mystic yet a great master. It won't be an exaggeration if I say Shri Siddheshwara Swamiji is the fusion these three personalities. His every sermon is so elevating that you will be placed out of time and space realms. I was introduced to Upanishads by this great master, whom we call 'Walking University'. And those Upanishads could clear all of my doubts that I had about the existence. I found most convincing answers. The answers that give us solace throughout the life.

In parallel to the spiritual quest, there was another enigmatic stream called 'Art' was running in me. When I came across Rabindranath Tagore and Kuvempu, I felt art is one of the ultimate instruments to approach the life. When the mind starts seeing beauty in everything, the heart fills with joy and the soul unfolds itself like a lotus of countless petals. Vedanta alone may seem a little dry for a non-sannyasin; the art pours nectar over that aridness and makes it green with full of divine flowers, spreading heavenly fragrance of an eternal ecstasy. The art has many forms and it is evolved over time. The Literature, Painting, Music, Sculpting and Photography, Cinema in recent times. Apart from the books, cinema is what I admired the most among all because of its inclusiveness. Then the same voyage of exploration was instigated eight years back. From Akira Kurosawa, Vittorio DeSica, Ingmar Bergman, Satyajit Ray, Alfred Hitchcock to Stanley Kubrick, Martin Scorsese, Steven Spielberg, Francis Ford Coppola, Abbas Kiarostami, Giuseppe Tornatore and to the recent favorite Christopher Nolan and so on. When I encountered Nolan, I intuited a synthesis of art, science and philosophy in his works and the creation of the art proves its significance at its best in all aspects. Nolan's work helped in the intellectual evolution of the viewer which is no less than listening to the Upanishads from a Maharshi (great sage) sitting under a serene tree in a forest.

My stance on the art is, it should not be a mere imitation of the nature but should disengage the mind from its imprisonment in the web of customary associations and routine ideas. If someone paints a tree exactly the way it is outside, I would prefer the real one! Art must bring light into the creator and the enjoyer of it, its ultimate aim must be aesthetic and intellectual evolution of man, it must help him find insights of truth. It is one of the responsibilities of the artist as well. Most of the films made by Nolan, serve that purpose. After watching a Nolan's movie, audience will be more intelligent than they were before entering the cinema hall. There is a seeker in Mr. Nolan himself, and the audiences also are carried along in his quest. In that way he creates a larger impact. For me, his career till date has seemed like an effort to prepare the entire world for leading a peaceful vedantic life!

In rural India there were numerous saints in almost all the villages, who used to deliver spiritual treatises every evening. Few talk of puranas(mythology) and few about Vedanta. After the advent of television and mobile phones, very few go to these speeches. At least, it was a break for the householders from daily routine life. Mind of a samsaari (mundane man) is always filled up with the material objects like business, money, house, children etc. In the evening congregations, they get a chance to forget all that and deliberate on the fundamentals of existence, the stars and the moons or the nature of life or the mind and the matter.

In a similar fashion, Christopher Nolan makes movies that give a break to ordinary routine life and make people think about the essentials of existence and astonish themselves. When we contemplate upon far off galaxies, black holes and neutron stars, the thoughts get matured and the mind grows broader. Then the idea of buying and reserving a plot of land for grandchildren looks absurd. This way Christopher Nolan helps people evolve and tap their potential to conceive their true nature.

One hundred years ago, there was an attempt by Shri Swami Vivekananda to unite both Vedantic idea of the existence and modern science. He had met Nikola Tesla for the same, and in a letter to his friend, swamiji wrote, "Mr. Tesla was charmed to hear about the Vedantic prana and akasha and the kalpas. He thinks he can demonstrate mathematically that force and matter are reducible to potential energy. I am to go to see him next week to get this mathematical demonstration. In that case Vedantic cosmology will be placed on the surest of foundations. I clearly see their perfect union with modern science, and the elucidation of one will be followed by that of the other", perhaps Shri Tesla could not infer a formula and this good news remained dormant and ephemeral. Now these ideas are getting renovated. Many quantum physicists agreed that all the manifested consciousness is originated from one universal consciousness. It is the responsibility of all human beings to understand the inclusiveness of the nature. A wise mind should try to recognize the oneness than debate over differences.

It is a need of the hour, to understand the cohesion of Art, Science and Philosophy. All the minds of the world are inherited from the same universal mind and there is no surprise, if a man in suits from London proposes a set of notions that are startlingly similar to the ideas of a long bearded sage in a remote cave of Himalayas.

We see how the religions are failed in 21st century; we see how the walls are being built between the minds of the people; we see how the east and the west are becoming a real life divisions than just in the maps; we see how the love is being replaced by animosity; we see how the gods have become expensive; we see how the human values are substituted by materialistic demands and needs. And a one stop solution for all these issues is art. The art is not yet completely adulterated, but pure here and there. It is the hope of future generations. It's time to lock the religious scriptures in an old suitcase for a while, until the modern man becomes matured enough to accept one another. Art is the universal religion.

I wrote this book because, I could not resist the gravitational waves received from far off galaxy, when a neutron star called art is collapsed into a black hole of spirituality. The waves travelled through the tunnel of wormhole called consciousness, resonated my soul. Everything is illumined, I could not resist...

Why should you read this book?

"Success of a book changes many lives, first being its author's."

– Author.

A rude answer for this question would be "You have no idea when you gonna die!" so you should know at least a little bit of it. No, I won't say this way, let's be diplomatic, Churchill said "Diplomacy is the art of telling plain truths without giving offense". All the animals except man are unaware that they are going to die someday. Is it a boon or a bane? When you have no idea of death, you just live, but will be deceived by the god sooner or later. Well, you and I are fortunate enough; God has revealed his plans to us. Therefore you must read this book. Here you and I are the same. We both are originated from the same energy! The breeze that kisses you in the morning walk touches me too. The sun who shines for you is a friend of mine as well. Now, when I write, keeping you in my mind, you are the motive and you are the writer. When I write with the intuition, god writes through me. So it's you and God co-authored this book. Where am I in between? As you are the author, you should read this book. The reader writes through the writer, and the writer reads through the reader.

If we try to put it in other way, the simple one line answer would be, one must read 'To know the secret of happiness and to be a yogi'. We all are here to enjoy and live this life as beautifully as possible. It is a great deal to know the secret of the same, and the secret is Vedanta. Once you know the secret, you would become a yogi, the moment you become a yogi, the life is all yours and this world is your playground. I ensure that you will surely be a yogi, by the time you complete this book. The process of writing about this sublime subject has changed my life forever. The perspective of looking at world is not the same anymore. I want to share it with you and introduce you to a yogic life, with an example. I want to hold your hand and walk the unexplored path together.

Shri Christopher Nolan is known for experiments in his films, the nonlinear story telling is vital among them. This book is also an experiment. It intends to provide an experience of Chris Nolan's film; there are surprises and twists like film plots. There is a spirit of avant-gardism as well. There are no rules or conventions, and expect abrupt cuts too. I do not think in English. I didn't surf through dictionary to discover some great literary words that are only understood by the writers or the words that woof and entreat to this world on my behalf to 'accept me as a writer'. No, I am trying to communicate to you like a bulk being from far off black hole through codes, and provoke you for an inner space journey. I am not a poet to aggrandize and glorify anything to increase its aesthetic quality. Nor am I a scientist to talk on facts and figures or comment on the plausibility of theories. I am an observer, and the work is the result of my reflections on my observation. When you read the complete book, I ensure that your world view will be changed about at least 5%.

The title contains ten chapters in total. The first chapter discusses on the fundamental problems of modern man in the philosophical sphere, which postulate the significance and inevitability of Christopher Nolan. The second chapter provides a brief introduction to his work. The third deals with the pulp of the book i.e. how Vedanta and Christopher Nolan's work are akin, and attempt to discover the same truth through different mediums and approaches. In the fourth chapter we try to understand the Law of feelings and emotions in a new fashion and how they are used in Nolan's films and also the way Mr. Nolan is helping in improvement of emotional quotient of the audience. The fifth chapter discusses on how Nolan is an artist with the spirit of science, factors that make him stand unique from other directors of the world. And the Sixth chapter contains an account of my interview with Christopher Nolan. The seventh chapter is about the concept of Yogi and explores on how Mr. Nolan himself fits to be a Yogi in personal and professional life, and how one can become a Yogi. The eighth chapter sheds light on Unavoidability of Art and Vedanta for the future of mankind. The ninth chapter discusses the solutions and talks about chasing the reality. The last chapter contains few random thoughts of the author about the topic, which were scattered here and there.

Chapter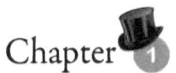

Why the world can't ignore Nolan

"Are you an atheist? Don't you believe in Christ? Well, that's fine. I would whisper in your ears, just believe in Christ-offered Nolan"

-Author

Everything starts with a question, even your reading of this book, you wish to ponder upon and nurture that question. A question is nothing but an idea in a rudimentary stage. We should ask questions, because only the questions can be asked. Answers are merely suggestive but not seductive like questions. Few questions that are unasked remain in mind and will go through an organic growth. Every question during its development in mind gives birth to many sub questions, but later on, changes its gender and becomes an answer! Thereafter it ceases to exist. All the answers are born out of questions, so they are dependent on questions. Therefore questions are great. Achievement of the man is his discovery of better questions every time in his quests for answers. Here is such a question "Why the world cannot ignore Nolan?" Oh what a question, does it really need an answer, isn't it palpable? There is 'World' in the question and Mr. Nolan himself. Here 'World' refers to all the people living in contemporary world (including North Koreans). Hence it involves everyone, even you and me. So why can't we ignore Christopher Nolan? This question also implies why Nolan is inevitable? And what is his significance in the present world.

There are some eternal facts which are apparent, like the Sun, whether we ignore or worship, Sun exists. He is unaltered at least for another 5 billion years. There are two classes of people in the world,

02 | Why the world can't ignore Nolan

those who live in an era and those who become an era. Aristotle, Gautama Buddha, Jesus Christ, M.K Gandhi fall in the second category. A wandering monk without complete clothing is worshipped by one third of the world, even after 2500 years of his departure. If anything that keeps a man immortal is, his thoughts. When men of such caliber live, they create a profound impact on the world that lasts forever. Their creation or the work provides solutions to many problems of the man. Whether we recognize or disregard, their work is universal. For example, Sun produces light, say there is a huge cave in an island, people who live there are ignorant of light, and their lives could be illuminated with the same sunlight. Similarly many problems that occur due to ignorance can be solved. We can either accept or reject such men, but we can't ignore. There is a famous dialogue in the movie 'The Departed', Frank Costello played by Jack Nicholson says, "I don't want to be a product of my environment. I want my environment to be a product of me." Few men live up to these words. Shri Christopher Nolan is one of them. The light has its relevance only when there is darkness. It is necessary to determine the problems or the issues faced by the modern man, before understanding the importance of Chris Nolan and his work. Else it may sound mere glorification and idolization of a man with no factual foundations.

Human being is distinct from other animals in terms of cognition, speech and intellectual capabilities. If we strike them out, man stands a primitive creature. We are evolved from the basic nomadic hunters to the sublime enlightened holy men. The reason and driver of this intellectual and psychological evolution is our mind. It is the reason behind all glories of human being. If man has to boast about any of his possessions or endowments, it is the mind. Through the mind he can elevate himself to be a god and can also be demoted to an animal. Mind is the reason for calling man an earth's child but heaven's heir. All the skyscrapers, literary epics, greatest musical compositions, philosophical volumes, spectacular films, path breaking scientific inventions are originated from the mind as a small thought or an idea. When the same mind is degraded, it could create disasters like world wars and nuclear weapons. Mind can transform a man into a Buddha or a Hitler. What a powerful and resourceful attribute of man it is! At the sametime, it is the most weak and volatile feature as well. If it does something repetitively, it will make it a habit, no matter whether it's good or bad. Since the very mind created the world around us, it likes its creation very much. Creator always loves his/its creation. Mind's own creations like most of the luxuries, variety of gadgets, internet, games, social networking have absorbed man into an inexorable blackhole of infotainment and posed serious problems.

Philosopher's grief:

First problem is 'strictly personal and nothing business'. We live in the 21st century, an era of slaves, mediocres and followers. What? If we stop by any philosopher, he will grieve the same with distress. Who is a philosopher? According to Greeks, philosophy is love of wisdom and philosopher is someone who is constantly seeking wisdom. He sees beyond what others see and not driven by the mind but uses it as a tool. He thinks deeply on any subject. After a deep thinking, he comes to a conclusion and proclaims his findings through a statement, like for example: Perfect is dead, Energy is an eternal delight, Love is that which lacks the object it seeks, and so on. He is an alchemist who can renovate the knowledge into wisdom. He might look peaceful, but he fights battles in the mind every moment. Once in a while he crosses the realm of mind and intelligence. Through his intuition, sometimes he sees divinely rays from the aperture in the ceiling of mind. He is one of the highest forms of humanity just one level down to the 'sage' or 'Yogi'. He is second from the top in the pyramid of wisdom.

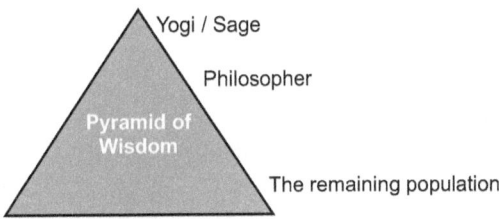

Figure 1.1 Pyramid of Wisdom

04 | Why the world can't ignore Nolan

A philosopher need not look weird with long hair and beard. He need not hang an identity around his neck as 'Philosopher'. He can be in anyone, a fisherman, a cobbler, an artist, a student, a household, an engineer, a doctor, a president or a scientist and so on. Only thing that makes philosopher distinct from rest of the herd is, 'He knows that he doesn't know'. He is aware that he is unaware of the inexplicable secret of existence and attempts to know it. The remaining classes of the people take things for granted. They just want to live because they have to live. They want to work because they have to work. They follow certain pattern, a stereotype from birth to death. From cradle to the grave, everything is so mechanical for them. They fear to cross the boundary line of the comfort zone. Sometimes they are afraid of truth. They fear solitude; they cannot confront themselves in the loneliness.

When a philosopher sees the humanity of today in his point of view, he might say 'there is everything uncanny'. He expresses pity on the modern man, who spends one third of his lifetime in using gadgets and in traffic. If we ask more, that philosopher might scratch his thick beard, and walk away screaming, "You slaves, mediocres and followers! Go find some enlightenment".

Philosopher's words always make sense, if not now, at least after decades or centuries. Post industrial revolution, that is, towards the end of 19th century, science was at its peak. Many machines are built to make human life easy. It continued further and after the advent of computers and smartphones, life of everyone on earth has been changed like never before. There is more impact of technology on human life in the last 2 decades than the past century. The graph of the change turned exponential.

Slaves:

There are two kinds of people living in the modern world: Independents and slaves. Independents create and slaves communicate. The slavery has many forms, we are slaves of gadgets and cannot live without them, we designed and built them to assist us in our day to day life, but they are our masters now. It's like protecting our own dog from the burglars in the night. Our days start with them, so they end too. We forgot the sun and the moon. We forgot the boundless universe and dwell in our own pockets, in the illusion that we are reaching far. Here's an excerpt from an online chat.

She: Hey whatsup, what you doin?

Me : I'm just sitting with my mom on terrace... talking, few memories.....and enjoying the evening. The silence....

She: Oh! That's nice. You said, you are clicking photos, just before 5 minutes?

Me: Yeah!, That's done. How about you?

She: I am helping my mom in the kitchen.

Neither I nor she is with our respective moms. We are not together either. And the time is just passing by like the newspaper guy in the morning, never waiting. Teenagers have started romance through online chat. Stickers have replaced warm hugs and kisses. Future generations might lose the sensitivity of touch and feel as well. We are so much absorbed that, we do not see in the eyes of the person sitting beside in subway train and too busy to acknowledge a smile, and even if smiles, it looks so synthetic.

Shri Einstein rightly said long time ago that, "I fear the day that technology will surpass our human interaction. The world will have a generation of idiots." And there is no doubt, here is that day. The proliferation of mobile apps are consuming most of the man hours. Slavery is a state, in which you cannot do what you wish. It is the same case. Mind cannot do what it really wants, due to its vulnerable feature of volatility. It just glances through mobile phone, clicks on something that leads to a different stream of thought in the mind. We simply go and open a social networking site to see if something interesting is there, though we are aware that, we are not going to find anything substantial. It is like peeping into our refrigerator once in a while, although we know that there is nothing special inside it. Every action that we perform gets recorded in our subconscious mind. It comes to the main mind again from the bottom in a round robin fashion. This helpless state is what we can term in general as 'e-addiction'. It is severe with many people who cannot live in the absence of internet.

Many of us defend gadgets and internet, saying that we obtain information and knowledge from them. That is true. We just acquire information, and accumulate it as knowledge, but not to the next level i.e. wisdom. There is a difference between Information, Knowledge and Wisdom. Information is facts and figures organized somewhere like Wikipedia. After reading it, our mind processes and remembers it in the form of memories which we call as knowledge. If we could discern, judge and create something out of knowledge, using intuition is Wisdom. In precise, it is the ability to see more than what our sense organs like eyes and mind can see. For example: 1) Our eyes see a beautiful architecture, knowing it as a building is knowledge and to apprehend it as manmade and it is a temporary object is wisdom. 2) The list of presidents is information. Knowing about who is president, what are his tasks and even thinking of how to become one is also knowledge. The view of, whether you are a president or the beggar, both are treated equally by the death, therefore one should seek something that conquers death, is wisdom. The wisdom springs from the tranquil mind and when we see things with immediacy, i.e. without any mediates. As soon as we drop off all our prejudices and presumptions, we become free. Only then we can grasp an apple as an apple. It is really a nightmare for the modern man to think of owning a quiet mind.

Many people used to joke, 'keeping offline from the internet is a luxury', but it is no more a joke or an embellishment. The outward journey of the mind has created a restless being, dissatisfied even if it gets what it desired for. Scrolling down the newsfeed or the updates of others endlessly without any goal will create a feeling of depression and mental fatigue. As stated in the beginning, what mind thinks repetitively will make it a habit. Social surfing accumulates depression day by day and that becomes a habit too. If Shri Charles Darwin was right, we might see human beings with abnormally big heads and long fingers soon in the coming future.

Followers:

Apart from the personal exposition, we use social media to follow our role models like film stars, politicians, artists, writers, sportsmen etc. There are two types of following, direct and indirect. If you like Mr. X, you follow him. If you hate Mr. X, you condemn him in every step, so you follow him indirectly. It's always good to have idols in life, that's how we grow, with their invisible influence on us; nevertheless we should think independently and choose. If you follow political party A or religion Z, why should your son follow the same? Why do you want to clone him in your own image? Why can't there be an intellectual freedom of choice? Why to build a cocoon for the next generation.

Most of the youngsters find joy in imitating their icons, it's nothing wrong, but there is again a serious risk. In today's era, anybody can become popular overnight. The character and the popularity need not be directly proportional. Many people watch reality shows like Big Brother or Big Boss. Strange and bizarre people for example, emotionally out bursting are also made participants to make the game more interesting, targeting more TRP to the channel. The people who sit at home are entertained by these men/women and unfortunately start following them. The Icons always influence their followers directly or indirectly. If those participants become drug addicts or attempt suicide, what about the followers? They might start thinking that, everything is normal and acceptable because our Icon does it and so on.

If we see this phenomenon of 'following' from a different angle, it's unduly perilous. It wipes out our capability of independent thinking; we no longer remain a human but a sheep. When we start believing in infallibility of our leaders or scriptures, and action according to them blindly, it would be another Germany of Hitler. World wars are the result of blind following of Nazis. The following is a sign of mass destruction in near future! In her popular novel 'Fountainhead', Ayn Rand writes *'Look at history. Everything thing we have, every great achievement has come from the independent work of some independent mind. Every horror and destruction came from attempts to force men into a herd of brainless, soulless robots. Without personal rights, without personal ambition, without will, hope, or dignity. It is an ancient conflict. It has another name: the individual against the collective.'* This system anaesthetically deprives men from the values like self-respect, liberty, dignity, freedom of thought and so on.

There is a saying in chapter 3 of Gita, for which there are multiple interpretations. But here it's quite relevant.

sreyan svadharmo vigunah paradharmat svanusthitat
svadharme nidhanam sreyah paradharmo bhayavahah

Its translation in precise will be, "It is better to live your own destiny imperfectly than to live an imitation of somebody else's life with perfection."

Do we really have to follow someone?

Mediocres:

Mediocre are those who produce anything ordinary. Only thing absent in the work of a mediocre is creativity. Everything becomes mediocrity when the creator is prejudiced. Creativity emanates when the mind is empty. However all the minds are filled with e-garbage, how can we accept creativity? For example, India is the biggest market for films. There are around 1.3 billion people in India. Still we see too many remake films made in mainstream and getting succeeded. Why? Films are made for money. How can there be anything extraordinary, when it's made for money or fame. Art has become another name for imitation.

If we see the news hour debates in TV channels, we feel annoyance and revulsion. There are more TV channels and reporters than the number of incidents worth calling news. Therefore, in order to remain in the competitive game, news is being created willfully, from the personal or private life of a so called celebrity or anything unusual that has the quality to grab attention of the people. Audiences have also started accepting such nonsensical junk as news.

In future, days might come where academic researches might lose their sheen. Now they are alive only due to few of the world-class universities and some god gifted minds. People might also start debating on the credibility and worthiness of Nobel Laureates which was usually not seen in the past. Increase in the number of remake films, rampant plagiarism, pointless discussions in news rooms, lack of progress in academic researches and so on, are the testimonials for an era of mediocrity.

After all he is a 'Philosuffer', he won't accept and praise the good people either. His grief continued. Who are these good people? A different category of matured individuals. They are career oriented and have read most of the success literature, not less than twenty personality development books. They aspire for growth and have ambitions in life. They strive for success. They are ready to sacrifice anything to become successful. So what is success? They say it's making fortune. That's all? No, Should have a minimum of 1 lakh followers in twitter, should be popular enough. That's all? No, should have opportunity to date someone whom they wish to; a few foreign trips and the officer in immigration should recognize their face and throw a smile at them. To achieve all this, they are ready to do anything. They work three forth of a day, they don't care even if they get heart attacks! They are fully motivated. They studied hard in school and college to get the high rank. They work harder to get the high rating. This is all fine. If somebody stops them and asks, what are you doing all this for? They do not know the answer. American author Edward Abbey says, 'Growth for the sake of growth is the ideology of the cancer cell'. It is unfortunate to the modern world that, being much educated compared to other classes; these people seem to be in a rat race. They are just climbing the ladder of success only to discover it's leaning against the wrong wall. They do not make any sincere effort to understand the fundamental questions like 'Who am I', 'Why I came to this world?', 'What am I doing here?', 'Where will I go once I die?' etc. According to 'Philosopher', every person should make an effort to understand all this; else what's the point in living this life as human being? Do we go to a movie without knowing at least the name of it? Then why not question about our beginning and end. How long one should live in this dream and illusion? How long should we be participants of this grand 'Truman Show'?

If we look at the condition of humanity from the aspect of politics, it's even more ill-fated. We all are being ruled by incompetent leaders who are intellectually unripe and lack in independent thinking. And we chose them as we don't have a choice. They all are just a mockery to the words like democratic, republic, by the people and for the people etc. We never know when North Korea launches a missile on Japan or America. We never know when the third world war will erupt (Its secondary that man is fighting many wars inside himself every day). If we keep aside our history of Korean War or the cold war politics and look at it afresh, there is no reason for North Korea to hate or wage war against USA. It's just the mindset of that juvenile leader with giant power in hand. He is an elephant in the backyard, never know when he will attack and vandalize. There is no one behaving responsibly to save the planet, international politics has become a game of 'Prestige'. An all-weather friend can turn a foe in one day. Most of the Medias are curious and expecting the war to happen. It shows the ascendancy of mass savagery.

We still read the news about hatred among whites and blacks, leftists and rightists. Communal riots, regionalism and aversion towards foreigners still prevail in few countries. If we try to find out the root cause for all this, it's the lack of thoughtfulness and immaturity in people. It's all ignorance. Education institutes are producing programmed robots every year, who just know how to get a job but not aware of how to live. The education system doesn't offer freedom for the expansion of soul or the progress of liberal thought but teaches some obsolete scientific formulas and social texts. If we still couldn't go beyond our racial and communal wells, how can we soar high and cross galaxies?

The world is religiously helpless. There are fanatics and proselytizing agents representing every religion. They promote fanaticism so they win. There are people who still believe in Hell and Satan in this modern era. What to say, except pity on them. Why can't they shatter the walls of that bastion built long ago by unknowns and open up to the mainstream world by being rational? Few religions still continued the approach of targeting the poor and converting them to theirs by applying a little butter on the victim's nose. How silly, how long are we going in this direction, being dependent on so called infallible scriptures? If Buddha, Zarathustra, Shankara, Jesus, Meera or Mohammed could know the truth, why can't everybody know it? They were human beings too, but they could transcend from being human to divine. If we still think ourselves as the sinners or the helpless followers, then who is going to help us? It is only we ourselves. Each of us could become another Buddha or Jesus. We are more interested and tend to like superstitions than the reality. We ignore what we see, what we experience and what we feel but believe what is written. If scriptures alone could get us the truth without the self-effort, then there would have been another Atlantis by now.

Other than the issues of well-being, if we cross the sphere of mind and try to go little higher and think the root cause of all this mess, we realize that it is alienation from oneself. The over intervention of technology into the lives of human being has created a serious problem of estrangement from the self (and obviously with the fellow beings). It is the mother of all problems and key factor of all these issues.

Most of us have begun identifying ourselves with communities and professions. This became a trend after the social media was introduced. I am a Hindu, I am Jewish, I am an Indian, I am an immigrant, I am a democrat, I am a social activist, I am a dalit, I am an engineer and so on. Here the 'I' is coupled with many other words and identities. When it becomes an obsession, there is a danger that man might end up in that illusion till he dies. Modern man forgot his own essence of manliness. Being a complex of 'Self' and material adjunct, he recognizes himself with Non-Self and carries on his daily life as the subject of knowledge, the agent of action, and the enjoyer of consequences of his action. Never inquiring into the 'I' which points to the self, he identifies himself with the body and sometimes the mind. With the body when he says 'I am fat' or 'I am short' and with the mind when he says 'I am depressed' or 'I am happy' and so on. Not only does he say so but acts on that basis. The true self 'I' is untouched from all these. Qualities like fat and short belong to the body; depressed and happy have their place in the mind. Ignorance of the self leads to alienation of self and in turn leads to multifarious suffering. This process of estrangement from self has made man a machine. The behavior is totally robotic, if you walk on the streets of Hong Kong, you will see a herd of people rushing to cross the roads holding smart phones in their hand. For a moment you will feel that you are in the midst of robots. Intellect is used only to gain material prosperity but not for the enquiry of existence. The self is obscured like the eclipsed sun.

To sum it up, the world is being swept away in the flood of information and newsfeed which is nothing but an e-garbage. Most of the human labor is being wasted for communication but not the creation. We are all intellectually lame and running a blind marathon with no target or whatsoever. 24 hours a day are not enough in today's busy life. It is still a matter of debate that whether we are consuming information or we are consumed by the information. All of these factors ascertain that The Philosopher is right. Plato said "There will be no end to the troubles of states, or of humanity itself, till philosophers become kings in this world, or till those we now call kings and rulers really and truly become philosophers". Now we are not in a condition to realize either of these cases, because the rulers hate philosophy as they are allergic to the truth. The philosophers hate politics because they don't like hypocrisy and the language of politics.

When the world is in an illusion or a dream, it needs a mass kick once in a while! A kick to awaken everyone, a kick to stop people and make them ask themselves what are they up to, and that kick is Christopher Nolan, he is the hope of our philosopher to save this mankind which is slipping through the blackhole of e-garbage and e-addiction, which is leading towards the alienation. Christopher Nolan touches every inner layer of human being and manages to propagate his thoughts effectively. Like, morally through The Dark Knight Trilogy; intellectually through Interstellar; and spiritually through Inception. Sometimes they are overlapped too. The scale in which he impacts is quite large as his efforts are not just confined to Hollywood but the entire world. The kick of Nolan is inevitable and impeccable. The people of the modern world cannot expect someone like Jesus Christ to be born and save them through his miracles. No! The modern prophets come in the suits with a corporate look, just like Christopher Nolan, a modern messenger!

Fistful of facts about Nolan

- Christopher Nolan (born July 30, 1970, London, England) was raised by an American mother and a British father, and his family spent time in both Chicago and London.

- His English father, Brendan James Nolan, was an advertising executive, and his American mother, Christina, worked as a flight attendant and an English teacher.

- Chris has an older brother, Matthew Francis Nolan(49) and a younger brother, Jonathan(41).

- As a child, he attended Haileybury, a boarding school just outside London.
  From a young age Nolan was interested in moviemaking and would use his father's Super-8 camera to make shorts.

- He made a stop motion animation homage named "Space Wars," at the age of eight, being a great admirer of the 1977 "Star Wars."

- At the age of 11, he aspired to be a professional filmmaker.

Chapter 2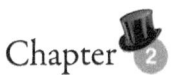

Doodlebug to Dunkirk

"Cinema is the most promising medium for instant enlightenment"   - Author

Cinema hall is another world, as most of us enter into it with all the curiosity and excitement. The way films are classified based on genres, moviegoers can also be categorized based on their demands and expectations from the films. Majority of them seek entertainment and the rest like the artistic aspects of the films; they pursue art and try to comprehend the films in that specific angle to find some beauty, insights and meanings that may lead towards the truth. In other words, spectators can be classified as 'Class' and 'Mass' audience. In most of the film industries, films are made targeting these sets of audience. It is a known fact that action, fantasy and sci-fi films have more chance to become box office success, because majority of the audience are the chasers of entertainment.

Every filmmaker has his own style of presentation. Most of them want to express and prove something to the audience. They basically try to understand the expectations and the heartbeats of the viewers and think on how to hold their attention till the climax, on how to satisfy them in different aspects of the film and so on. Here the true seed and motivation for the film is audience, director is separate from them. Such filmmakers strive hard to create a 'wow' factor in the craft. After a relentless hard work, they present it someday like a showman on stage, well! They succeed. The other kind of directors, make films for the sake of filmmaking. They have a story to tell, not bothered on whether the audience will accept or reject it! They just tell the stories, because they love it. Just the way nightingales sing from the bushes in moonlight, in a remote forest.

Cinema is the art form that went through more experiments than any other art. As we know filmmaking is telling stories, the story can fall into any genre, suspense thriller or a love story, a war film or a family drama, it is a story. Everyone has a story but, how you portray it to the audience is what the art of Cinema all about. The simplest way to connect to audience is through emotions and difficult approach is through intellectualism, there is a possibility to blend both of them as well. It is to educate and uplift the emotional quotient and intellectual vigor of the audience. This is what is done by his holiness Shri Christopher Nolan.

Intellectual gymnastics :

Those film directors who try to make intellectual films, challenge the audience, whereas Mr. Nolan challenges himself. He wants to see an interesting film, so he makes it on his own. He relies on fiction, because imagination is your own world, and you have the freewill to exploit it in every possible way. Hence he designs a cobweb (a web for Dom Cob!). He traps the characters and audience in it and conveys them the rules of the game through some clues (these rules may not be genuine). Gradually audiences become familiar with the situation. He makes sure that the audiences see what the protagonist sees and they feel what he feels. Now the game begins, how to escape from this cobweb, audience wants to escape along with the characters; here the beauty is the characters help the audience in this exertion. In the course of this break out, characters ask questions and try to find out answers but never allow audience to become self-conscious. The characters and audiences are deceived, during this process. After traversing through the maze, viewers are not given a conclusion but an eye-opener kind of climax. For a moment it gives an ephemeral relief, but it is a trigger for the further expedition. It continues in the mind of audience even after coming out of the theatre.

This is the reason we do not just know the story of Nolan's films but experience them. When we experience something, it remains in our very being, not just the mind. In this way, we are very much influenced by such films. Assume that Inception film is not made yet, and someone tells you the story of it. How will you receive and digest it, It will surely sound ludicrous, it would look amazingly complex and something deep. You would say, it's just possible in the imagination. But what we see in the film is the same complexity but yet comprehensive. Nolan's films are visual labyrinths that invite you to go deeper into them and will not promise that you will go out.

When we watch the trick of this magician closely, there is one common thread throughout all his works, a tussle between subjective experiences and the objective reality. The characters are suspicious about the empirical world around. In few scenarios he mimics that, what we see could be false and truth could be something else. He brings that panic feeling in the audience and conveys them that they are trapped in this very fundamental paradox.

Many people argue that Nolan employs gimmick with nonlinear narration and ambiguous endings, but it's the style of storytelling. It comes from within, not forced. It's already engrained in his mind and soul. When you try to force the style or form, it might turn to be a pitfall too. Conventions in the filmmaking are just the confinements! One should break them occasionally. Whatever Tarantino tried in 'Pulp Fiction' inspired many film makers. 'Close Up' of Abbas Kiaroshtami looks like a low budget docufiction, but it's a great experiment that highlights the thin line between a drama and documentary, audience are forced to change their perspective once in a while, and makes them utter 'Brilliant!' at the climax, the film is considered as one of the finest film crafts. Materializing the idea is important than the forms and conventions. If you give a direct conclusion to the audience, it would be less art and more of preaching and proposition. Art should ignite your intellect and emotions. Insights arrive only when your mind knows the tactics of tryst with the light within. The conflicts and gaps are very much necessary in art because the source of expression itself is imperfect, and filling the gaps with their own imagination is a great feast to the audience too. Cinema becomes more engaging and interactive when it makes its audience involve in the story and provoke them to complete the maze by their own.

Few movie goers comment that 'Nolan uses lies and deception as the key element in his films. He misguides the audience in the beginning and they realize it later'. Yes, it is the expected quality of an artist. If you just tell anything naturally how could it be called an art, rather than imitation. Lie keeps you awake and attentive about the plot, because you don't want to be cheated again. Nolan uses mostly dark backdrops and less light just to keep the attention of the audience towards the screen in the movie house.

Such a giant talent of Christopher Nolan had a humble beginning. Journey was started in London with an 8mm camera gifted by his Dad. He decided to become a professional filmmaker when he was 11. Like every other filmmaker in the world, Nolan too had made short films that went unnoticed, like a hidden poem or a first love letter in your secret diary. Tarantella and Larceny are among them. Doodlebug is the first short film which is known to the world as his first. We need to know about the works of Nolan in brief before trying to understand him deeply. Here is a list of works; they are not reviews nor the analysis but a brief introduction and appreciation.

Doodlebug(1997):

Anybody could guess about Nolan's future glory if they had watched this short. Doodlebug(1997) is a 3 minute short film produced by his then girlfriend and future wife Emma Thomas. The story concerns a grungy man, in a dim lighted filthy apartment. He is anxious and paranoid, trying to kill a small bug-like creature that is scurrying on the floor. It is revealed that the bug resembles a miniature version of himself. He squashes the bug with his shoe. However, every movement the "Doodlebug" makes, is later matched by the man himself and he is later squashed by a larger version of himself.

The film can be interpreted in many ways with a deep symbolism. One can say that the protagonist is trying to wipe out his memories and traumas of the past. And in that process his current actions are also getting converted into past and the whole effort is turning futile.

Another interpretation would be, man is trying to achieve something blindly at the cost of his life itself. For normal movie goers, the film amuses by portraying a lonely man with psychological complications. There is surely a sprout of 'Nolanism' witnessed in this film.

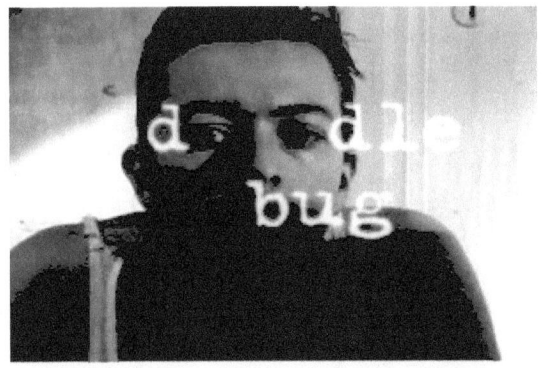

Figure 2.1 Doodle bug   (Courtesy of Nolan Family)

Following(1998) :

Chris Nolan came into limelight by his first feature 'Following' in 1998, which he personally funded and filmed with his friends. 'Following' depicts an unemployed young writer (Jeremy Theobald) who trails strangers through London, hoping they will provide material for his first novel, but is drawn into a criminal underworld when he fails to keep his distance. The film was said to be inspired by Nolan's experience of living in London and having his flat burgled: *"There is an interesting connection between a stranger going through your possessions and the concept of following people at random through a crowd – both take you beyond the boundaries of ordinary social relations"*. 'Following' was made on a modest budget of £3,000 and was shot on weekends over the course of a year. To conserve film stock, each scene in the film was rehearsed extensively to ensure that the first or second take could be used in the final edit. Co-produced with Emma Thomas and Jeremy Theobald, Nolan wrote, photographed and edited the film himself. It garnered him many international acclaims. People responded well saying that, it's a psychological thriller and a pure Hitchcock style classic; it not merely entertains but shocks you by showing another style of burgling with bizarre fantasies of burglars. It makes you worry and think what if you were the targets. To put it in a single line, 'Following' paved the way for Nolan's entry into Hollywood.

The beauty of Following is, it looked so professional and of great quality that, nobody would believe it's a debut of a director or a low budget flick. In every frame of the film, Nolan's meticulous attention for the craft and hard work could be seen. He used natural lights and guerilla shooting technique for few scenes. Regarding the casting, he took best out of his friends.

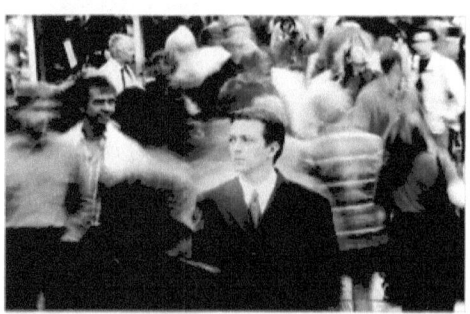

Figure 2.2 Following   (Courtesy of Nolan Family)

Memento (2000):

Based on a short story written by his brother Jonathan, Chris wrote the script and Emma managed to get funds for it. The protagonist is played by a non-celebrity actor Guy Pearce. Guy stars as a man who, as a result of a past trauma, suffers from anterograde amnesia, the inability to form new memories and suffers short-term memory loss approximately every five minutes. He is searching for the persons who attacked him and killed his wife, using an intricate system of Polaroid photographs and tattoos to track information he cannot remember. Memento is presented as two different sequences of scenes interspersed during the film: a series in black-and-white that is shown chronologically and a series of color sequences showed in reverse order (simulating for the audience the mental state of the protagonist). The two sequences meet at the end of the film, producing one complete and cohesive narrative.

Being a modest budget film but of a great output, it won two academy nominations for screenplay and editing. Here, Nolan tries to play with memories and belief system of audience. It is conventional and a normal tendency to believe whatever the narrator in the film narrates. But in this film Nolan proved it false. The protagonist is unreliable. Unlike his other movies audience are deceived instead of characters in the film. It is rare of this kind and he takes a chance to test audience by showing same scene twice. The film amazes with its extraordinary screenplay and nonlinear narration. What happens when you cannot make new memories and you have mission to complete? is the core theme of plot. And the way of its representation is remarkable. Audiences are forced to be in the shoes of protagonist and experience his subjective mental imbalance. It is revered among the film fraternity as a modern classic psychological thriller and one of the best films of 2000.

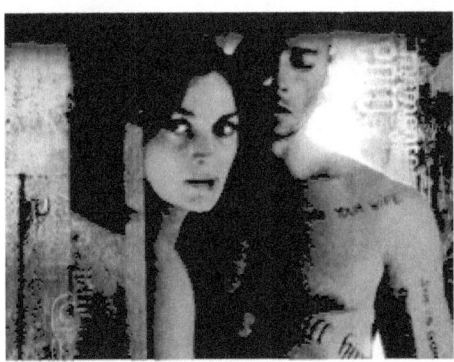

Figure 2.3 Memento poster scene (Courtesy of Team Todd)

Insomnia(2002):

Nolan got a chance to work with Hollywood legends like Al Pacino and Robin Williams through this film. It is a remake of the 1997 Norwegian film of the same name. It tells the story of two Los Angeles homicide detectives investigating a murder in an Alaskan town. The investigation goes horribly wrong when detective Will Dormer (played by Al Pacino) mistakenly shoots his partner and subsequently attempts to cover up his bungle. The title of the film refers to his inability to sleep; the result of his guilt (represented by the relentless glare of the midnight sun).The film is very much symbolic.

Though it's a remake, Nolan had his signature in the film with sharp dialogues and the locations that sync with mood; aesthetics that take audience beyond the story and renders an experience of arctic life. The guilt, fatigue and psychological struggle of the protagonist leave audience mentally uncomfortable sometimes. That's how Nolan achieves his objective.

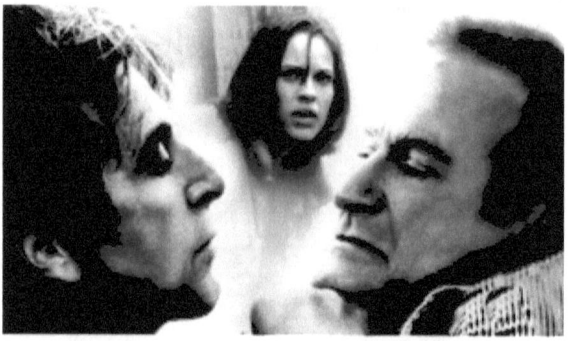

Figure 2.4 Insomnia poster scene (Courtesy of Alcon Entertainment, Witt/Thomas, Section eight productions)

The Prestige(2006):

It is a mystery thriller film adopted by Jonathan Nolan, from the novel of the same name by Christopher Priest. It is a story of two rival stage magicians Robert Angier and Alfred Borden in London, at the end of the 19th century. Obsessed with creating the best stage illusion, they engage in competitive one-upmanship with tragic result. It is interesting to see Nikola Tesla played by David Bowie in the movie.

Prestige is a multilayered metaphorical film. The more you "Watch it closely" the more you be astonished by the tricks of magician Nolan. It's a metaphor for his own life as a Hollywood director, every filmmaker is a magician. In the movie, Robert Angier says "You never understood why we did this. The audience knows the truth: the world is simple. It's miserable, solid all the way through. But if you could fool them, even for a second, then you can make them wonder, and then you... then you got to see something really special. You really don't know? It was... it was the look on their faces..." These lines apply to both Nolan as a director and The GOD or the creator of this existence. The dialogue "Are you watching closely?" is repeated multiple times in the movie, which is purely symbolic and it in turn makes audience unconsciously conscious along with the characters. 'Prestige' is indeed a prestigious adventure of Nolan.

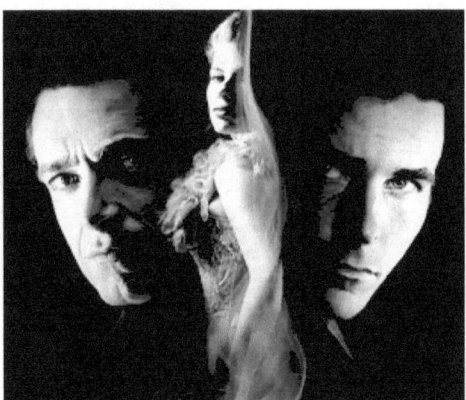

Figure 2.5 The Prestige poster scene (Courtesy of Touchstone Pictures, New Market Films, Syncopy)

Dark Knight Trilogy:

It is a set of three Batman movies. It includes Batman Begins (2005), The Dark Knight (2008), and The Dark Knight Rises

(2012). It is considered as the best ever super hero film series in the history of cinema with a great critical and commercial success. With an ensemble star cast and grandeur, Nolan gave a completely new dimension to the characters that were already a house hold names. Though there were many films made before with vigilantism as a theme, what Nolan portrays is very distinct from them. Without glorifying the hero unnecessarily, gives importance to all the characters in the movie. Else we wouldn't remember Joker, mighty Bane, Commissioner Gordon, Harvey Dent and Scarecrow etc. All of these characters have their own weightage. Another important thing to consider here is, crafting the story of Batman in Gotham city that looks relevant in this technological age. However Nolan succeeded in it, even introduced Nuclear Power in the wrong hands of Bane in the last installment of the series. It looked like a symbolic mockery of future Kim Jong Un but Bane is far better, though a villain, he gains respect to certain extent.

Many serious issues like economical imbalance and moral values, ethics are blended within the story and as Mr. Wayne himself says "Idea was to be a symbol and Batman could be anybody", Batman was just a symbol to be good and do good in modern era.

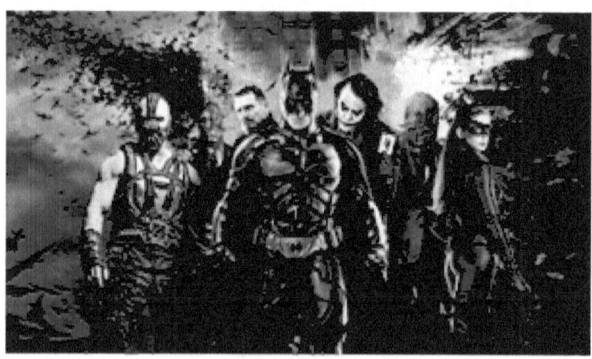

Figure 2.6 Dark Knight Trilogy
(Courtesy of Legendary Pictures and Syncopy)

Inception (2010):

It's an original heist thriller movie by Nolan that left the whole world perplexed. Protagonist played by Leo Dicaprio, a professional thief who steals information by infiltrating the subconscious and is offered a chance to have his criminal history erased as payment for a seemingly impossible task: "inception", the implantation of another person's idea into a target's subconscious. Cob along with his team takes the target to deeper levels of dreams and performs inception. They achieve it in the deepest possible level and the film is all about how this fascinating mission is executed.

It is a unique sci-fi thriller and rare of its kind. Nolan succeeded in making the audiences adaptable to take the concept seriously while watching the film. He taught much of the psychology to layman unconsciously and stealthily through this film. This movie is so infectious, that it is debated widely till date in many forums. Its climax is still an unsolved mystery, though Chris says, Cob is in his subjective reality. Nolan himself has done an inception into the minds of audience through the Inception.

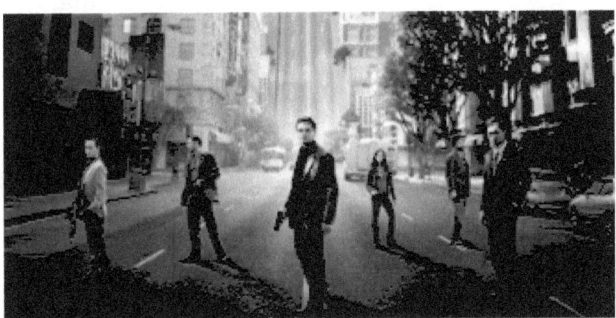

Figure 2.7 Inception (Courtesy of Legendary Pictures and Syncopy)

One should honor Chris Nolan for treating audience smart. No other director on earth could have made this film in a comprehensive manner as he did with the most complex story. Inception is the best work of Nolan in his career and path breaking movie to come out from Hollywood in recent past.

Interstellar (2014):

Set in a dystopian future where humanity is struggling to survive, it follows a group of astronauts who travel through a wormhole in search of a new home for humanity. Nolan teamed up with his brother Jonathan and the physicist Kip Thorne, to render the people a scientific thrilling experience with authentic science but not mere imagination. When we say a Sci-Fi, there's more a fiction than science but Interstellar stands an exception to this notion. Chris and team made science accessible to the normal man without a science background with a spectacle. This movie is scientific, artistic and philosophical treat as well, a great fusion of all this revolves around emotions coupled with Nolan's intuition. Audience were excited to know the truth of the universe with a space tour of interstellar and also they are convinced that only love is eternal and it's the only medium that can surpass time and space to communicate from one dimension to another. Kip Thorne, The Nobel Prize winning theoretical physicist and scientific consultant for this movie has written a book called 'The Science of Interstellar'. It is worth a read for those who want to understand and clarify the doubts sprung in mind after watching the film.

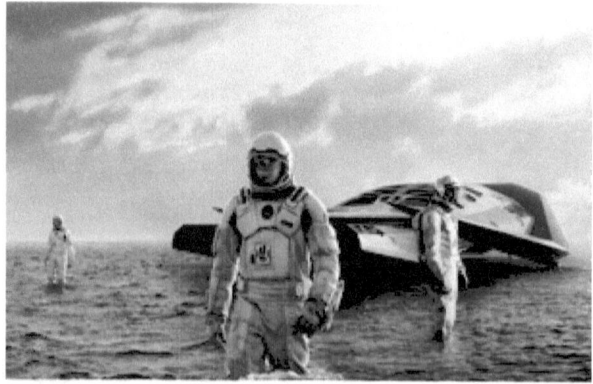

Figure 2.8 Interstellar (Courtesy of Legendary Pictures, Syncopy, Lynda Obst Productions)

Dunkirk(2017):

It is the first non-fiction work of Nolan. The film depicts the story of 'Dunkirk Evacuation' of World War II. It portrays the operation from three perspectives: land, sea, and air. Dunkirk has little dialogue, since Nolan sought to create suspense from cinematography and sound. It was shot with IMAX 65MM camera to create a real-time experience. Chris had intended to create a feeling for the audience as if they are sitting on the long stretched sea along with soldiers, through a wide huge screen and he succeeded in it. Though he consulted Spielberg by referring to 'Saving Private Ryan', Chris had made it clear that, he will not treat it as a war film but a rescue film. It talks of humanity in the midst of bombing sounds as well as the chaos of war. Nolan's approach to depict it in three ways makes sure that the audience will be placed in a cockpit for a while before switching to a ship or sea shore. It gives a comprehensive view and the story as a whole and hence everyone feels satisfied because he/she missed nothing to know. Nolan played with the time again, the timelines of all three viewpoints of the story are different, but it's edited in such a way that we get equal experience of all of it.

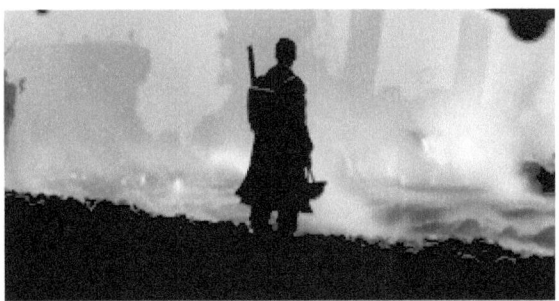

Figure 2.9 Dunkirk (Courtesy of Syncopy Inc)

Fistful of facts about Nolan

- During his college years, Nolan made two short films.

- The first was the surreal 8 mm Tarantella (1989), which was shown on Image Union (an independent film and video showcase on the Public Broadcasting Service).

- The second was Larceny (1995), filmed over a weekend in black and white with a limited cast, crew, and equipment. Funded by Nolan and shot with the society's equipment, it appeared at the Cambridge Film Festival in 1996 and is considered one of UCL's best shorts.

- After attending University College London, where he studied English literature, Nolan began directing corporate and industrial training videos.

- At the same time he was working on his first full-length release, Following (1998).

Chapter

Vedanta and Nolan Cinema

"If you think you know, you don't! If you think you don't, you are dumb!"

Thousands of years ago, when the man was still a nomadic hunter in the west, he was thinking about the world very seriously in the east, especially in India. He started asking fundamental questions like, is it all real that appears to me? Or is it different from what I perceive? Why it is changing? Will it be there forever? Was it always there in the past? Is there nothing which doesn't change at all? And so on. He was not much worried about his bread and milk. There was no one to acknowledge his queer doubts, as he was the first ever man to ask these ultimate questions. He began his quest to find the answers and was obsessed with it. Over a period of time he understood that he cannot see the unchanging truth with the changing eyes. On realizing that he cannot see or perceive what lies behind this existence with his sense organs, he went into the forest, spent his days and years in solitude and observed the world very keenly. Reflected on what he saw, used his intelligence and tried to analyze it with rational thinking and logical reasoning, ended up becoming a philosopher. It did not appease him. Sooner or later he crossed the boundaries of intelligence and found a method called 'Yoga'. It took him beyond the domain of intelligence and philosophy. He became a 'Yogi'. His ultimate invention was, "The Mind has got a great power". It can see more than the eyes and knows more than the intelligence. This power is called intuition or a direct perception or an immediate knowledge without any medium of sense organs. For example, I see a tree with the help of organs like eyes and mind using all the predefined knowledge that my mind accumulated. The moment I see the tree, I identify it with all my botanical knowledge, its leaf color, flower pattern, species etc. And then comes my likes or dislikes about it from the same source of memories. Therefore all the knowledge that I get out of thoughts and feelings is mediate, but how about my-self? 'I know that I am there!', 'I know that I exist' how do I know it? Without the help of my eyes or mind, 'I know that I am'. I experience that 'I' exist and the whole world is the object of my perception. There comes the light! He realized the true nature of the 'self' and of this entire existence. He conquered the myth. He understood that the seer and the seen are one. The results of his experiments proved that there is immanent divinity in man and it could be revealed with the help of yoga. This glorious man wished to propagate this knowledge for generations to come. He recorded that wisdom in the scriptures called 'Upanishads'. We call these scriptures collectively as Vedanta.

In the modern world, at least once in our entire life, we are likely to encounter the questions like 'Who am I', 'Who sent me here?', 'What is this existence all about?' , 'Where will I go after death?' , 'Is there a way that I can be immortal?' , 'Are gods and angels real?', 'What are dreams?' , 'What is the nature of my mind?', 'Are the mind and intellects same?', 'Is there anything beyond the mind?', 'How is this universe created?', 'Can I elevate myself to be a god?', 'What is evolution?', 'Is the universe mortal or immortal?', 'Why god created this universe?', 'What is consciousness?' etc. For most of them our modern science cannot answer. But our ancient Indian science can answer all of these questions with rational and logical analysis in an appealing way.

Vedanta literally means the end of 'Vedas'. Vedas are four in number and they contain elements such as liturgical material as well as mythological accounts, details on practice of rituals, mantras/hymns to praise and please the gods, in order to get a certain boon (which is still a materialistic idea). Present day they are mostly obsolete. Terms Vedas and Vedanta are being used interchangeably. We are more interested in Vedanta than the Vedas. Vedanta contains Upanishads; we can say Vedanta is nothing but interpretations of Upanishads. These are written in Sanskrit, they are possibly the highest level of intellectual and spiritual discussions about the nature of human existence and the universe. A great German philosopher Arthur Schopenhauer rightly says, *"It is the most satisfying and elevating reading which is possible in the world; it has been the solace of my life and will be the solace of my death"*. Upanishad literally means "Sitting next to Guru" or "Closer to God". The exquisiteness of these scriptures is, they are written in most engaging manner, as the deliberations between a guru and his disciples. The disciple asks the question which arises in the mind of the reader. And it is answered by the Guru, after listening to the answer reader is equally satisfied as that of the disciple. One more interesting and astonishing fact about the Upanishads is, for most of them, authors are unknown! Those who wrote these volumes are so selfless that they just wanted wisdom to be propagated but not the names. Unlike every other scripture, Upanishads do not revolve around glory of a man or god, but the thought, principle is emphasized than the idolatry. The holy book of Hindus, Bhagavad-Gita and 'Brahmasutras' (summary of Upanishads written to clear all conflicts and systematize the doctrines) are inherited from the Upanishads. These two texts along with Upanishads form 'Prasthanatrayi', meaning *Three Sources* of Vedanta Philosophy.

Upanishads are so influential that, three lines from one of them changed the life of a great yogi Debendranath Tagore. Being the son of a prince, Debendranath was brought up in a lap of luxury surrounded by all pageantry of palace. As he grew up, his view point towards the world changed completely pursuant to the destiny. The silent observation of the stars one night on the bank of Ganges beside his grandmother's death bed filled his mind with wonder and the thought dawned on him that the grand universe that he saw before him could not have proceeded from any finite being. One day in a state of extreme misery, he noticed a stray leaf of a book flying past him; he picked it up and started reading it repeatedly not less than ten times. It was the opening verse of the Ishopanishad which said *"God is immanent in all things, in whatsoever lives and moves in the universe; enjoy therefore without being attached; covet not wealth belonging to the others."* From that day his course of life was changed forever. This Maharshi Debendranath is the father of great mystical poet and Nobel laureate Shri Rabindranath Tagore. This great transformation in the life of his father must have made a profound influence on Shri Rabindranath to become such a divinely poet.

Paul Deusson, one of the chief German philosophers and friend of Frederic Nietzsche says, "*Whatever may be the discoveries of the scientific mind, none can dispute the eternal truths propounded by the Upanishads. Though they may appear as riddles, the key to solve them lies in our heart and if one were to approach them with an open mind one could secure the treasure as did the Rishis of ancient times*". There is no end to the list of people whose lives are illumined by the wisdom of Upanishads.

Upanishads are 108 in numbers. Few prominent ones that can be listed are, Mundaka, Mandukya, Ishavashya, Aithreya, Chandogya, Thaitthiriya, Kenopanishad, Kathopanishad, Prashnopanishad. Though all of them profess the same truth, approaches are different and vividly mesmerizing. They are neither to be mugged up nor to be written and kept. They are just to be experienced either by reading or by listening from the masters.

Many sages and scholars interpreted these Upanishads in their own ways and established different schools of philosophy. There are mainly three different schools under the umbrella of Vedanta namely dualism (Dvaita), non-dualism (Advaita), qualified dualism (Vishishtadvaita). They just differ in the interpretations of the texts. It doesn't mean that Advaita is incompatible to Dvaita, latter is only one of the three steps. The first is dualism and then the man gets to a higher state of partial non-dualism. And the last he finds is one with the universe. Therefore the three do not contradict but fulfill and settle at one ultimate truth.

Dvaita (Dualism):

Sub-school was founded by the 13th-century scholar Madhvacharya. It believes that God (Vishnu, supreme soul) and the individual souls(jivatman) exist as independent realities.

Vishishtadvaita(Qualified nondualism): Ramanuja was the main proponent of this school and it postulates qualified nondualism - that ultimate reality(Brahman) and human soul are different but with the potential to be identical. It is non-dualism of the qualified whole, in which Brahman alone exists, but is characterized by multiplicity.

Advaita(Nondualism):

Though its roots trace back to the 1st millennium BCE, the most prominent exponent of the Advaita Vedanta is considered by the tradition to be 8th century scholar Adi Shankara and it posits non dualism - that ultimate reality(Brahman) and human soul are identical and all reality is interconnected oneness. The term Advaita refers to its idea that the soul(true self, Atman) is the same as the highest metaphysical Reality(Brahman). The followers of this school seek spiritual liberation through acquiring vidya(knowledge) of one's true identity as Atman, and the identity of Atman and Brahman.

All of these schools have accepted the ultimate truth and they play around the common belief in different paths. If an Indian preaches anything, it will be Advaita Vedanta, right from Buddha to Basava on to Ramakrishna all preached Advaita Vedanta without mentioning it explicitly;

What Vedanta preaches?

There is a universal consciousness that pervades everywhere throughout all this creation intrinsically and externally. Our inherent consciousness (soul) is the part of same one universal consciousness. Goal of human life is to realize it, get rid of the animal like attitude and rise to a sublime level, where the human being reveals his divinity and becomes immortal. In precise, "Man is born out of Brahman or the god, there is an implicit godliness in him. He is already divine, and the goal of this life is to realize his immortal nature and divinity." Swami Vivekananda asserts Vedanta in a nutshell, *"Each soul is potentially divine. The goal is to manifest this divinity by controlling nature, external and internal. Do this either by work, or worship, or psychic control, or philosophy - by one, or more, or all of these - and be free. This is the whole of religion. Doctrines, or dogmas, or rituals, or books, or temples, or forms, are but secondary details."* Vedanta doesn't intend to create any belief system, but it is purely practical. It affirms, 'know your-self, In order to know the Brahman'. As we are aware, the nature of Brahman is Sachidananda (sat+chit+ananda=> existence+consciousness+bliss) and we are inherited by the same absolute universal principle, our nature is also identical to that of sachidananda. If we just imagine and don't make an effort to watch over the mind, the whole idea will turn into romanticism. Many well taught scholars never experience due to over burden of the accumulated knowledge. One need not carry the yacht over his shoulder, but should be left at the shore as its purpose is achieved. Every once in a while, from moment to moment, if we watch our mind and live consciously, we are already leading a vedantic life. Vedanta turns our attention towards the self, experience the self and then be the very experience.

Vedanta & Nolan's films:

Christopher Nolan's movies seem like Vedantic experiments on large masses of the people. There is a striking similarity between both of these approaches of Vedanta and Nolan's Cinema. Both are paradoxical towards the truth and both do not either accept the truth or reject it, but they manage to make audience experience a glimpse of it. It hypothesizes, Nolan agrees that the truth can neither be conceived with sense organs nor it could be expressible through words, but it is a subjective experience that everyone has to go through. If we conclude on either of the viewpoint, that is, for example: god(truth) exists or god(truth) doesn't exist, it is like we are creating belief system and that belief system is the very first hurdle to the seeker of truth. If we say god exists, our search ends by satisfying and accepting an imaginary fact (How can a fact be imaginary!). The mind likes beliefs because it need not struggle. The other case, if we believe that god doesn't exist, and then we know, the entire effort is futile. So there is no point in searching anything, eat and sleep attitude will be formed. So it is wise and the only way to keep the spark alive.

"True words seem paradoxical" says Lao Tzu. Right from the beginning of his career as a filmmaker, Christopher Nolan's approach was suspicion and paradox. Film as a paradox around fiction, a labyrinth for audience; nothing is served in the silver plate. There is deception all through, only the deception can make audience face and question themselves and make them alert and attentive. This deception leaves an impression on the mind; the chaos remains even after coming out of the theatre. Man becomes more attentive and conscious even in his daily worldly business. This serves the very purpose of deceiving characters. It helps gradually shatter all the long lived resilient walls of belief in the mind. Deception is just a way but not the approach in the story. However the approach is paradoxical. In the film Inception, everything is paradoxical. That is the very reason it could create a lot of thinking in the viewers. We are unclear, whether the hero is in dream or reality even till the end. It seems like even the entire movie is a big dream of Dom Cob during the course of his flight journey back to home. Nothing is certain and nothing can be accepted (Nolan uses concepts like Penrose stairs, an impossible object in constructing the dream world, which seems real but not). In the film Memento, we are unsure that whether Leonard Shelby is truthful and honest or the killer of his own wife. In the film Insomnia, audiences also feel the same guilt and dilemma as that of Will Dormer for an accidental killing of his associate cop (due to the unclear vision in the fog). It remains a mystery throughout the film

and audiences are unsure of whether it is a 'willful' murder out of professional jealousy or just an accident. It just happens in the fog. It is proven that 'viewers' of Nolan's films cultivate an attitude of contradiction and suspicion towards the truth, which is a great instrument for the real-time quest of ultimate truth. The ultimate paradox that Chris Nolan had used is in Interstellar. It is the circular timeline of Cooper's life. Here we struggle to figure out, whether Cooper is currently a bulk being in fifth dimension and goes back to his past or the farmer Cooper is going to be a bulk being in the future to save the humanity. Cooper is in the black hole tesseract and sending messages to Murph (and the farmer Cooper!) to go to the NASA facility. Cooper could be in blackhole, only if he went to NASA facility before! It remains an eternal quest to the audience. The paradox remains unsolved, even though we think time as the 4th dimension and could be manipulated anywhere anytime in its linearity. Paradoxes are meant to be that. When the mind is exposed to such a visual paradoxical closed loop, the blunt edges of the mind will be sharpened.

In the entire Vedanta, the truth or the Brahman is accepted as the form of Satchidananda but never defined and expressed or objectified in any certain way, because the words or the language fail to do that. The perception of mind and the language are in the lower strata and the Brahman is all together in a different realm. A Chinese monk says, *"The moment you express the experience, it becomes a lie"*. The ultimate reality can't be expressed but to be experienced. It is the subjective reality as in the Nolan's movies.

In Kena Upanishad, the sweetest among all, there is a dialogue between the master and his disciples. It has the following lines, 1:1) Who sends the mind to wander afar? Who drives life to start on its journey? Who impels us to utter these words? Who is the Spirit behind the eye and the ear? 1:2) It is the ear of the ear, the eye of the eye, and the word of words, the mind of mind, and the life of life. Those who follow wisdom pass beyond and, on leaving this world, become immortal.

1:3) There the eye goes not, nor words, nor mind. We know not, we cannot understand, how he can be explained: He is above the known and he is above the unknown. Thus have we heard from the ancient sages who explained this truth to us. Going further the master says something like, if you say you know it, you don't! And if you say you don't, you are dumb! This riddle will create a process of rational churning in the mind and will lead to an experience of its own kind, an insight.

In Taittiriya Upanishad, we see a chapter about creation, though initially it seems illogical, we realize its sublimity only when we try to perceive it from the heart of a surrendered humble disciple. "He created all this-whatever there is. Having created all this, he entered into it. Having entered into it, he became both the manifested and the unmanifested, both the defined and undefined, both the supported and unsupported, both the intelligent and the non-intelligent, both the real and the unreal. The satya became all this: whatever there is. Therefore call it the Truth."

(Since we used masculine gender to address the Brahman, It doesn't mean we should a form of some Hindu god or anything, It is just symbolic. The Brahman is neither male nor female and he is both.)

In Isha Upanishad, Brahman is explained as "One unmoving that is swifter than mind; that the gods reach not, for it progresses ever in front... That moves and that moves not; that is far and the same is near; that is within all this and that also is without all this." Since the universe or the existence is a pattern of contradiction, a web of paradox which no intellect top-heavy rationalization is able unravel, there is no other approach that could be used other than the discussed. This enigmatic technique itself enables one to find and experience truth. In this way we can say, Nolan a Brahmarshi preparing viewers to perceive the paradoxes of the Upanishads. There are other aspects in this preparation; we can choose two films of

Nolan to discuss on them, Inception and Interstellar.

Inception:

To put it in one line, it is a story of stealing ideas of others through dreams and planting new ideas in other's mind through the same means. When we look at this film from the Vedantic perspective, it achieved in making the audience take first leap of faith towards the evolution of man. Nolan succeeded in taking an entire generation to the next level of progression. (We shall understand what we mean by evolution here, later in this chapter). I say Inception is a prerequisite for studying and comprehending Vedanta. The first and foremost question that stimulates everyone to explore spirituality is 'Who am I?' So every one of us knows and understands, 'I am not just the body', because 'You' are the one who is reading, not your body. We frequently say 'I am trying to build my body' so here I said, build 'my' body, hence I is different than the body. Next thing is 'I am not the mind', though most of the times 'I' represents the mind or mind represents the 'I', the mind and I are different, because 'I know what I am thinking'. Here the thinker is mind and the knower is I. In the movie, audiences are invisibly influenced and subconsciously made aware, that 'I' am different than the mind. This is the first leap, a leap of faith in the path of Vedanta.

Despite knowing this, being literates we say, 'I am moody now' or 'I am depressed' or 'I am angry' etc. But actually if you analyze, it is our mind but not us. The thought that's arisen in the mind has created that feeling of depression. So mind is depressed, not 'I'. In the movie, hero Cob, many times reiterates, 'My subconscious', 'His subconscious' etc. This very notion forces the audience to firmly believe that 'I' is different than the mind. Since it is said repetitively, the idea gets imprinted in the subconscious of the audience making them more matured.

Now, what is mind? Mind is a bunch of thoughts. If there are no thoughts, there is no existence of mind as such. Scientists and yogis have found out that, there are two layers of mind i.e. conscious and subconscious mind. Conscious mind is what we always think and work with, whereas subconscious mind records each and every impression that 'I' am coming across. And these impressions are called memories. Memories are stored and buried deep down in the subconscious mind. From their depth, they sometimes come onto the surface like bubbles in the pond. Few people use the word, 'Karma' for this phenomenon. Since each and every thought and action are recorded in our subconscious mind, whenever anything related or similar thought is encountered in conscious/main mind, that hidden thought resurfaces and the main mind starts churning it. Even for the audience with non-psychological and non-science background, Inception teaches about conscious and subconscious mind unconsciously.

Mind contains thoughts. So I want to know what is there in other's mind, without letting them know about my extraction. In order to do that, I need to know about his thoughts/ideas. Best possible way to do this is, know about his dreams. Dreams are nothing but pictorial images of thoughts screened to us, when we are slept. Mind functions even when we are asleep, so it keeps on thinking about some random topic no matter whether we are awake or slept. If I am obsessed with something or whatever that I think more will manifest in my dream. So dreams give a clue about what are my thoughts/ideas. Then how to navigate through other's dreams? Via shared dreaming. When we navigate through other's dreams, we see their world. We see the people and objects in their life. We literally experience their subjective world, their likes and dislikes as well. Taking all the elements into consideration, one should design a plan to harness the subject's mind and plant an idea.

In the film, the idea of showing the subconscious of the subject, defending from intruders or any suspicion is really brilliant. Now the next leap, Inception of an idea into another's mind i.e. sowing the seeds and making it grow into a gigantic tree with unparalleled branches is the real challenge. Cob does it with his gang through multilayered deep dreams. In that process also the story is too wise, in order to make subject's mind adapt to it so easily, Cob and team chooses more subtle way by invoking sentimental relationship between father and the son.

The remaining details are pure cinema. However the real takeaways from the movie Inception in the Vedantic perspective are,

- 'I' am not the body and 'I' am not the mind.

    The film preaches unconsciously that, 'I' am not a gross body of flesh and bones, I am something finer! Right from the beginning of the movie, there is no scene that demotes viewer to feel that they are merely the body. In a metaphorical sense, they are floating in a higher level i.e. all of them are sitting in a flight from Sydney to Los Angeles flying 35000 feet high from the ground.

    The logic used in the film implies that body is a mere vehicle. When your body dies in a deeper level of dream, you would be transported to the upper level. With the same notion, assume what happens when your body dies in the level 0, that is, in the current reality! (What would have happened if 'Cobol engineering tails' killed Cob?) You should be carried to another level where you don't have a body, a shift from gross matter to finer form. But still, you exist. The movie symbolizes that body is a mere vehicle to carry you.

    And the mind is in the body. Mind is the inner body and body is the outer mind. The finer moves the grosser; engine moves the whole train; mind moves the body and same way the mind chooses the body when it goes out of it. Buddha says, 'You become what you think'. The fascinating thing here is, Cob says we need to plant an idea into Fischer's mind, so Fischer is not his mind!

- I have a mind and its made up of two compartments, conscious and subconscious.

Subconscious mind has a property of awareness, parallel perception and all the accumulated knowledge and experiences till date. When Cob takes Ariadne for a trial tour in his shared dream, we see the projections of his subconscious mind. We also notice that, in the first level of mission Inception, i.e. Yusuf's dream of a rainy Los Angeles, Cob and team abducts Fischer, but they are attacked by armed projections from Fischer's subconscious, which has been specifically trained to defend him against such intruders. Through these scenarios, viewer's subconscious becomes aware of the fact that, there is a subconscious mind and it can be trained as well.

When 'I' see the world and process in the real time of 'here and now' is the main mind, which keeps on thinking of any thoughts after a stimulus from the objects it observes or feels. Few people remember their old school days when it rains; the fragrance of the soil makes them nostalgic! In India schools open in June that's when the monsoon/rainy season start. In this case, with the help of sense organs like eyes and nose, main mind perceived rain. All the experiences about the rain, rush into it from the subconscious. Isn't it beautiful? When we watch TV while eating, the subconscious helps us eat, by instructing hand to carry out, to and fro from the plate to mouth and the main mind is busy watching TV.

✦ Mind is just a tool and it can be used, manipulated and customized.

Mind exists when there are thoughts in it otherwise it has no explicit existence. The mind is nothing but a bunch of thoughts. Therefore if we consciously chose those thoughts, mind becomes our slave. We should keep watching on it with a sharp axe, the moment an unnecessary thought sprouts up, we should cut it mercilessly if we want to use it as a tool. We behave as per the society we are surrounded by. Parrot in the butcher's house yells, 'Bring him inside, chop off his head'. Sibling of the same parrot which grew in the house of a saint says 'Please come inside, kindly relax, and accept our small offering'. All minds are influenced from the world. The influence is nothing but the deep impression on mind. If we have to change the behavior of butcher's parrot, we need to educate and influence him with the attitude of saint, until his former influence goes so deeper in the stack of subconscious that it cannot be reachable by main mind.

- Dreams are nothing but the pictorial representation of thoughts of a mind.

  Inception teaches us that, we dream on what we have already thought. There is a hodgepodge, but every single element of what we see in dream is already experienced. Dreams also indicate that our mind functions even when we are slept.

- Thoughts stored in subconscious mind in the form of memories come up once in a while; it can be due to any external catalyst/triggers. If it repeats, it becomes an obsession for example: Cobb's case. He struggles to get rid of the memories of Mal and his guilt hounds him every time he remembers her. The more he remembers, the more he suffers.

- Possibility of entering into another person's mind.

  We have seen many mystics and magicians who can read through the mind of others. In Vedanta, there is a separate discipline called Rajayoga to achieve this practically. The secret here is, it is the same universal mind that everyone is sharing. This universal mind is just like an ocean, all individual minds are waves. If we know the nature of water in one wave, we know the entire ocean. On account of this continuity of mind, the thought can be transferred and read.

However, planting the idea or the inception and its success totally depends upon the nature of the subject's mind. Therefore, the objective is to plant the idea in the subconscious, so that it endures.

A stimulating thing to recall here is, sometimes you sing a song and your friend says, she/he is thinking about the same song in her mind. Or there are times when you think of something deeply and someone comes to you and talks about the same thing.

✦ There is a portrayal of a state of the mind/consciousness called 'Limbo' (in the realm of dream); it is an infinite space of raw subconscious, an unconstructed dream space.

In Vedanta, we have four states of consciousness, being wakeful (jagrat), dreaming (svapna), deep sleep state (sushupthi) and Transcendental (turiya)/pure consciousness. The Limbo can be compared with the sushupthi, where the mind ceases its physical and mental activities and absorbs into itself. In this state, the person will be at complete rest and happiness, as the mind is silent, there are no dreams observed.

An intelligent reader might get a doubt here like, is it really the state of sushupti? Or it is a state something like coma? Well no, in the state of coma, consciousness is absent. Where as in the states of Limbo and Sushupti there is infinite consciousness and only the mind is quiescent. For example, if Mr. Saito was not brought back from Limbo, he wouldn't be unconscious, but would have ended up insane in the movie.

✦ The last and most advanced is, the quest for reality.

The Climax of the movie is the true essence of vedantic spirit, questioning the reality. What if this 70 odd years of life is also a dream? Am I awake or dreaming a grand dream? How can I make sure that life is not a dream or illusion? In ancient time, this very question made many family men to go into forest and reflect upon the thoughts and understand the nature of this existence. Christopher Nolan is the actual Dom Cob of real life, who has planted an idea and succeeded in inception into the minds of audience and that simple idea is 'Is this phenomenal world real?'. When everyone stands up from his/her seat after the climax, a spark of questioning attitude and an idea passes through their minds, because Nolan cuts before the top falls and when it is still wobbling. Though Cob is in his own subjective reality, we are not yet sure that whether it is still a dream or waking state. We as an audience could even think that the entire movie itself is a dream of Dom Cob when he sleeps in the flight while travelling back home. One more dimensions in this debate is, movie projected in the cinema hall is also a dream, cinema is also a kind of illusion and dream. That's the reason few say, the theme song used for kick has lines 'I regret nothing, no, I have no regrets...I don't care of the past anymore, I set my memories on fire....'. The song provokes audience to think that they are in dream and the song is a kick to wake them up (running time of Inception is 2h:28m and the Edith Piaf's original song duration is 2m:28s, is it a coincidence!?).

This concept of illusion has a great deal of debate and deliberation in Vedanta. It's called 'Maya', 'that which exists, but is constantly changing and thus is spiritually unreal'. Vedanta describes the universe and the human experience, as an interplay of Purusha (the eternal, unchanging principle, consciousness) and Prakruti (the temporary, changing material world, nature). The former manifests itself as Atman (soul, self), and the latter as Maya. Vedanta refers to the knowledge of Atman as 'true knowledge (vidya)', and the knowledge of Maya as 'false knowledge (avidya)'. Brihadaranyaka Upanishad, describes Maya as 'the tendency to imagine something where it does not exist, for example, atman with the body'. Maya pre-exists and co-exists with Brahman - the Universal

Consciousness. Maya is perceived reality, one that does not reveal the hidden principles, the true reality. Maya is unconscious, Atman is conscious.

Svetasvatara Upanishad, summarizes the concept as, the Brahman (Supreme Soul) is the hidden reality; nature is magic; Brahman is the magician; human beings are infatuated with the magic and thus they create bondage to illusions and delusions. For the freedom and liberation, one must seek true insights and correct knowledge of the principles behind the hidden magic.

Gaudapada in his Karika(Collection of philosophical poetry) on Mandukya Upanishad explains the interplay of Atman and Maya as follows,

> The soul is imagined first, then the particularity of objects,
> External and internal, as one knows so one remembers.
> As a rope, not perceived distinctly in dark, is erroneously imagined,
> As snake, as a streak of water, so is the soul (Atman) erroneously imagined.
> As when the rope is distinctly perceived,
> and the erroneous imagination withdrawn.
> Only the rope remains, without a second,
> so when distinctly perceived, the Atman.
> When he as Pranas (living beings), as all the diverse objects appears to us,
> Then it is all mere Maya, with which the Brahman
> (Supreme Soul) deceives himself.
> Gaudapada, Mandukya Karika 2.16-19

Sarvasara Upanishad refers to two concepts: Mithya and Maya. It defines Mithya as illusion and calls it one of three kinds of substances, along with Sat (True existence) and Asat (false existence). It defines Maya as all what is not Atman. Maya has no beginning, but has an end. Maya declares Sarvasara, is anything that can be studied and subjected to proof and disproof, anything with Gunas or the qualities. In the human search for Self-knowledge, Maya is that which obscures, confuses and distracts an individual.

In other words, Advaita Vedanta philosophy says, there are two realities: Vyavaharika (empirical reality) and Paramarthika (absolute, spiritual reality). Maya is the empirical reality that entangles the consciousness. Maya has the power to create a bondage to the empirical world, preventing the unveiling of the true, unitary Self or Brahman. The theory of Maya was developed by the ninth-century Advaita Hindu philosopher Adi Shankara. However, competing theistic Dvaita scholars contested Shankara's theory, and stated that Shankara did not offer a theory of the relationship between Brahman and Maya. A later Advaita scholar Prakasatman addressed this, by explaining, "Maya and Brahman together constitute the entire universe, just like two kinds of interwoven threads create a fabric. Maya is the manifestation of the world, whereas Brahman, which supports Maya, is the cause of the world." Vivekananda said, "*When the Hindu says the world is Maya, at once people get the idea that the world is an illusion. This interpretation has some basis, as coming through the Buddhist philosophers, because there was one section of philosophers who did not believe in the external world at all. But the Maya of the Vedanta, in its last developed form, is neither Idealism nor Realism, nor is it a theory. It is a simple statement of facts — what we are and what we see around us.*"

In our case, Cob is trapped in a very complex web called Maya. Hence Inception stands as a true prerequisite for the spiritual seekers of the modern world.

Interstellar:

Interstellar seems like a sequel of Inception to a Vedantin. After a deep inner journey in the quest of the truth, its outer expedition ignited by inner intuition. The science behind Interstellar like black holes, wormholes, space travel, Time, relativity are well explained in detail by the Nobel laureate and great physicist Kip Thorne in his book 'The Science of Interstellar'. The movie is more science and less fiction, and more intuitive than intellectual. Like any other space sci-fi movie, it has an objective for the protagonist to be achieved, but with possibly more authentic science than other movies. What stuck audience the most is, the concept of fifth dimension and Nolan accepting love as a medium like gravity to communicate between the dimensions.

Any theoretical physicist has to be a philosopher, or else he cannot produce such great truths. It's evident that Albert Einstein was influenced by Frederic Nietzsche and was himself a philosopher. Einstein had deeper insights about the life in a wider scale than just the science. His heart beated for the entire humanity. If you are a mere philosopher you shall only feed your intellect in the cost of whole being. Other aspects of heart and moral nature are left starving. Christopher Nolan is not just a philosopher, but a poet in himself.

After the fourth dimension called time, we have one more possible dimension in the movie and people who are living in that state are called 'Bulk beings'. With respect to Vedanta, that higher dimension could be Brahman! Or eternal consciousness spread throughout the universe. A state which is unaffected by the time and space and something that is separate from these dimensions. Brahman pervades through, and transcends the entire universe, but can be realized only when we surpass the realms of time and space. In the film, Cooper was shown in bodily form trapped in the tessaract, but it need not be that way. Since the body is bound by time and space, how can it be present in 5th dimension, but for the understanding purpose we have Cooper shown that way. When you go into a higher dimension, time is just another lower level, which you can even manipulate.

Vedantic Involution and Time Paradox of Interstellar:

There is an eternal debate about the creation, though most of us have accepted Big Bang to be true, we are unsure about what was there before Big Bang? Is time started from the time of Big Bang? In that case, the question, what was there before Big Bang will become meaningless, because the word 'before' itself is pointing towards the past which in turn points to time. So what was there before Big Bang?

Vedanta offers an appealing answer to this question. The evolution is existent forever and it is based on cause and effect pattern. Something cannot be created out of nothing. At least in our current view of science, all the energy and matter is in equilibrium. We cannot take out some joules of energy out of the existence; it can just be transformed to another form. Universe is created out of nothing will seem very illogical to any intellectual. There is nothing that is produced out of nothing.

Vedanta proclaims, all this evolution was there already in the finer form, but manifested later, entire creation that we see today was already preexisting in the originating single point. Swami Vivekananda explains it beautifully with a seed and tree example *"Out of what has this universe been produced then? From a preceding fine universe. Out of what has men been produced? The preceding fine form. Out of what has the tree been produced? Out of the seed; the whole of the tree was there in the seed. It comes out and becomes manifest. So, the whole of this universe has been created out of this very universe existing in a minute form. It has been made manifest now. It will go back to that minute form, and again will be made manifest".* As per the Involution theory, evolution is just the manifestation of the preexistent in finer form. Therefore this existence is eternal and infinite. Now the universe is in its expansion face, so some day it will start with its contraction journey. A Big Bang will be followed by a Big Crunch. After a certain extent of time, the speed of expansion of the universe may not exceed the escape velocity, and then the mutual gravitational attraction of all its matter will eventually cause it to contract. A blackhole collides with another black hole forming a big blackhole and it in turn collides with another, swallowing the planets from its mouth of event horizon. A huge blackhole might be formed and its space-time singularity ends up with a Big Crunch singularity. So again a Big Bang, then the quarks, atoms, galaxies, suns, moons and then you, me, Donald Trump and so on.

Now, why is it difficult for us to conceive and believe that existence is infinite? Because we are habituated with time. We go for a movie, it has 2 hours of duration, and it has a beginning and an end. A book has the first page and the last, our body has certain age, our pets and the buildings too. So, there is a preconception in our worldly experienced mind that, everything should have a beginning and an end. Whatever it may be, it should start and end. What happens if we step outside the realm of time? We become infinite beings because we are not affected or aged out by the time. So we will be bulk beings. For the Cooper's case in Interstellar, who is sending the signals from the blackhole tesseract to his daughter Murph and to himself: if you be in the shoes of bulk beings and observe, it is not at all a paradox, but if you remain in lower brane and think as a normal man, it looks like a paradox. The director takes the audience to the next level of life form in evolution, the immortal beings. If we just say it in words, it will sound ludicrous for the spectators, and may not be effective as the mind will not be harnessed for it, but in the film, audience go through the very experience of it. The experience of infiniteness is really needed to accept the ultimate truth of existence. Paradoxes are meant to experience but not to be memorized. True experience comes when the mind is not busy creating memories. Devine things look paradox to the human beings but it is the very nature of bulk beings or the immortals. Brahman revealed himself to Cooper and Cooper revealed himself to the Brahman, because Cooper is the Brahman, who never said Aham Brahmasmi!

Apart from the science, the takeaways from the movie in a vedantic perspective are:

- The impact of time on our existence.

    Time is something that can't be defined, the oxford dictionary meaning goes like, *"the indefinite continued progress of existence and events in the past, present and future regarded as a whole"*, but it doesn't appease us. We are sure that empirical existence is bound by the time. Time causes change. If the time is not understood as a dimension, we tend to think that aging out is the basic nature of creation and there is no way out of it. It can move in either of the direction, the evolution or devolution. We may not agree to accept the concept of devolution, because we are in an evolution phase now.

In the Film we see daughter Murph is aging out faster than the Father Cooper. Murph has grandchildren and almost on death bed by the time her dad Cooper meets her. We are aware that the gravitational time dilation effect of general relativity is the reason for this. When you go to a planet where there is more gravity than the earth's, time slows down! But nothing looks abnormal from astronaut's frame of reference. It is like, Cooper is in a train and Murph is in a flight, both can play with ball, move around and do whatever they want, everything looks normal from their perspectives and frame of references, but the speed that they are moving and distance that they are covering in space differs. Now if we think, train and flight are in the different planetary gravitational fields, and assume that train is in the planet having more mass and gravity, the time slows for Cooper. Though he feels everything is normal, his rate of movement in time is slower compared to that of Murph's, where the value of gravity is less. Lighter the faster, light the fastest.

Matter is bound by the time, but we are not just the matter, we are non-matter too. The Consciousness that we possess is not bound by the time. It was the same when I was a child. And will remain the same when I grow old, a constant and timeless phenomenon. Now, the wisest at the same time, stupidest question one can ask is what would happen if there were no time?

- Possibility to escape the dimension of time.

  The bulk beings in the film are out of the realm of time and who can actually alter the timeline. Proposition of this new dimension and theory, postulates a new direction of thinking, what could exist beyond time and space. And the rishis of ancient India have proclaimed to the world, thousands of years ago that, only the god/ truth/ Brahman /universal energy/consciousness exists beyond the time.

- Curiosity about existence.

Every space travel is initiated out of curiosity about the cosmos. And this curiosity triggers many questions about the existence. The way metaphysics suggests for the inner journey to reach the truth, the outer journey also is destined to realize the same truth.

- An idea of immortality (the ultimate goal of a yogi)

Man has the potential to become immortal and he is born to realize that very prospective. It is the ultimate state of the yogi. There are accounts of great yogi's like Mahavatar Babaji, who is living in Himalayas from past 2000 years. Many people in different timelines of the history have claimed that they have met him. The ultimate goal of humanity is to escape the realm of Time.

- Science alone doesn't help to seek the truth but the heart and mind driven by the intuition.

Interstellar is made with both head and the heart; reason and faith. It is more humane than technical. It advocates, intuition is more imperative than the reasoning. Science has its own limitations. It helps you merely to perceive and study the objective world. Science keeps mum when it is challenged to simulate an individual's psychic experiences or the subjective viewpoint; it fails to understand the consciousness and the intuition. Quest for reality is incomplete without metaphysics.

- Love is something that can transcend time and space.

  Speech of Brand, in the movie about love has a great philosophical essence and value. Here it goes *"love isn't something we invented - it's observable, powerful. Why shouldn't it mean something?"* and Cooper brings her back to the normalcy by saying *"It means social utility - child rearing, social bonding"* but Brand doesn't bend so easily, she replies *"We love people who've died. Where's the social utility in that? Maybe it means more - something we can't understand, yet. Maybe it's some evidence, some artifact of higher dimensions that we can't consciously perceive. I'm drawn across the universe to someone I haven't seen for a decade, who know is probably dead. Love is the one thing we're capable of perceiving that transcends dimensions of time and space. Maybe we should trust that, even if we can't yet understand it".*

  Cooper, from the tesseract tries to communicate to his daughter Murph through signals of gravitational anomaly. Only love could kindle him to do that. It is very interesting to know, that Vedanta embraces 'Love' as one of the ways to realize the Brahman. In Vedanta, love is a medium to transcend these dimensions of time and space and to reach the dimension of eternal consciousness or the Brahman. It is one of the four paths of spiritual practices called 'Bhakti Yoga' other three being 'Jnana yoga' the path of reasoning and intellect, 'Karmayoga' the path of work as worship, and Rajayoga the path of a strict yogic discipline.

  Bhakti Yoga is all about love and admiration. Love the god, love everyone and everything around. When you love everyone, you see yourself in everyone and the love embraces you from all around. When I start thinking everyone as myself and do not discriminate, an unconditioned love blossoms, since everyone and everything is made up of the same one Brahman. It will lead to a unity of 'I' and the nature or 'I' and the Brahman.

In Brihadaranyaka Upanishad, Yajnavalkya says to Maitreyi "*A wife loves her husband not for his sake, but for her own sake. A husband loves his wife not for her sake, but for his own sake. Parents love their children not for the sake of the children, but for their own sake. People love wealth not for its sake, but for their own sake. Thinkers and teachers are loved, not for their sake, but for the sake of the Self. Warriors and kings are loved, not for their sake, but for the sake of the Self. The Gods, the worlds, the beings in the world, and everything else - they are not loved for their sake, but for the sake of the Self. Indeed, you must realize the Self. Hear it, reflect upon it, and meditate upon it.*"

When we start seeing the divinity in others, our love towards them becomes unselfish, motiveless and pure which will lead us to the truth. The path of love or the Bhakti yoga is the most appealing for mass population because, love doesn't need any formal education or literacy, but a pure heart. Many illiterates (in the sense of unlettered) in India got enlightened by following the path of Bhakti Yoga and have become great yogis. Bhagavad Gita also upholds Bhakti Yoga as one of the prime paths to realize truth.

Interstellar is a magnum opus. For every kind of audience, the film stretches certain kind of transcendental experience. A scientist will see it in a different angle than that of a philosopher or a college student and a filmmaker. After crossing through the wormhole and traversing the planets,

Cooper enters the most enigmatic, fascinating, gigantic Gargantua black hole. It can be used as the metaphor to the death. The same amount of fear, inquisitiveness, thrill and a sense of freedom is experienced by Cooper, as soon as he enters the blackhole. Nobody has ever entered into the blackhole and experienced that journey; nobody knows the experience of death as well. It's the most intriguing part of the life, science and art. Interstellar throws a platform to experience the inexperienced and make us get used to it. Lastly we see it as a doorway to the different world and life.

Interstellar is not merely subjective experience but a rendezvous of Chris Nolan with the Brahman. Nolan has invited everyone from the west and east yet again to the Vedantic journey knowingly or unknowingly. And those who have watched these movies have already made half way through. There is no doubt that a day might come in future where there is a mass enlightenment movement during the times of Buddha. Go into a dark hall, come out enlightened.

Fistful of facts about Nolan

- He is married to Emma Thomas, who has co-produced all of his films.

- He met her when he was just 19 years old, during his days at the University College of London.

- They have four children - Flora Nolan, Rory Nolan, Oliver Nolan and Magnus Nolan.

- The duo have together founded the production company Syncopy Inc.

- He currently resides in Los Angeles with his family.

Chapter

Law of feelings and emotions

"Why do we suffer? Because we do not ask this question while suffering!"   - Author

There are many ways to connect to the audience through the medium of motion pictures. Few go with grandeur entertainment using spectacular visual treats; some creators rely on their story, script and narration; whereas several filmmakers try to touch the intellect of the people and make them think; and rest all depend upon the emotions. Every human being has emotions, literates and illiterates; rich and poor alike, so it is the best and easy way to connect. Nonetheless, are emotions good? How can we judge whether they are good or bad because they are inevitable, is there a difference between emotions and feelings? Apart from what science and psychology talk about them, is there any real meaning? Or can any meaning be real?

Many critics complain that Chris Nolan's movies are emotionless. They say, 'we do not feel' too much while watching his films (Ofcourse! We think instead); audience don't get empathized with the characters; there is no emotional depth in scenes etc. Well, the emotional depth is framed when there is an organic development of the characters, by portraying their personality traits, behavior and their background etc. Everything in the film 'The Godfather' is etched into the hearts of audience because all the characters are constructed very carefully in a detailed manner; however what one should observe here is, the plot is an advantage for this process. Since it's a family story, it's somewhat easy to build up the characters and drive them emotionally. Michael was in marine corps, honored with a medal of bravery in world war, loved his Dad and the entire family but his Dad was brutally attacked, he was humiliated, and also wanted to prove that he is not a cute college boy but a grown up and can do big things! All of these factors drove him emotionally to an extent where he shoots Sollozzo and McCluskey in the point blank range to avenge his wounds. 'The Godfather' is very rich in terms of emotions. In the contrary if we take the example of Dom Cob of Inception, we don't know much about him as a man; he is an expert in extraction and was a good architect, that's all. When he struggles to survive with and forget his deceased wife Mal, audience doesn't empathize much, like that of the characters in 'The Godfather'. Obviously we don't feel much for an unknown person when compared to a loved one or a relative. In the case of 'The Godfather' characters drive the story, where as in Inception, the story drives characters.

But what are emotions, character bursting out into tears every so often and making audience the same? Or the heroine having wild sex with an unknown? Or a gangster shooting a guy suddenly for fun? What emotions we want. One should apprehend that, Nolan's films are feeling-full. In this context it's essential to understand what we mean by the Feelings and Emotions. There are three kinds of people in the world: 1) With Feelings 2) With Emotions and 3) Composite (With feelings and emotions). Just like the good, the bad and the ugly:

Feelings:

Feelings are smooth and tender for the mind and are pleasant for the surroundings as well. Feeling is a constant phenomenon, when we say 'I love roses' or 'I like reading', we don't feel like squeezing and biting the rose petals, because we have lot of love towards it. If we do that, that's emotion. Feeling of love is distant yet so close; it's an unceasing admiration and devotion. If we lose that flower, we will not go insane or commit suicide, it's just gone, that's all. We love that flower even in the absence of it, because the love never changes according to the target objects. The feeling won't lead to any catastrophe.

The man living with feeling is serene and his/her mind is tranquil and unruffled. There is no abrupt action or a sudden reaction. All the situations are handled calmly with grace. Such men are so composed and are full of peace and love. For such people, life is just another version of heaven. For example: Gautham Buddha, M K Gandhi, Jesus Christ etc. all of them had deep love towards the humanity and they lived with feelings. Nobody saw a Buddha crying or Jesus beating someone in anger or Gandhi shouting on people. They knew the truth of being happy, they behaved with full of feelings.

Now, is it good to live with feelings? Yes, it is, if we want to be happy. What we work for? Why do we go on an excursion? Why do we do shopping? What is this all mess for? To be happy, yes! The simplest way to live happily is to live with feelings.

Now, how to live happily or how to live with feelings? The finest way is to watch on our thoughts and behavior. Once we start watching on our own thoughts and hushing down the unnecessary ones, mind will begin to be quiescent. Once the mind is serene and peaceful, we turn out to be happy, happiness is the byproduct of peaceful mind; the swans will start swaying on the lake of the mind. Everything is silent and full of love and compassion. But there are very less people of such caliber.

Emotions:

The next category of the people is those living with emotions. They are the most dangerous creatures. They react suddenly and shock others, not healthy for the self and society. It's a big weakness for them; most of them are prone to habits like drinks and drugs. Their mind is not constant. 80% of the crimes are committed by such emotional people. They are unaware of what they are going through in that very moment. They take sudden decisions and repent later. If the emotional person is well cultured and a writer or an artist, he starts preaching that, being emotional is noble and great. He glorifies his own weakness as a great expected quality of man. An emotional writer forms a group of readers and followers who are also emotional and starts fooling them. It's because readers/audiences are easily attracted towards someone who is similar and he can easily strike the chord of their emotions. Subsequently such groups turn into a psychological epidemic in the community, which will lead to increase in the number of crimes. They are likely to become the reason for domestic violence, organized crimes, and accidents. Emotional people are also prone to commit suicide. Being emotional is a real threat.

In very rare cases like that of great painter Vincent Van Gogh, Mathematician Ramanujan or Gurudatt the director of movie 'Pyasa' who is revered as the Orson Welles of India (he actually looked and lived like poet Dylan Thomas! Startling coincidence is both drunk heavily and both died at the young age of 39). If you are emotional and equally genius, you will be devoted to your work or passion so emotionally, that you will forget the world and yourself. The passion will turn into an obsession and you will start bursting from inside. You become a fountain of intuitive art and produce remarkable results, but will end up soon. The life will not last long for emotional people.

The best example to distinguish between feelings and emotions is the Lake and Ocean. Lake is not moving, always calm and serene, non-catastrophic and also it doesn't produce much energy. Whereas ocean is made up of gigantic waves, it's never calm and unpredictable. It can bring tsunamis, the same way it can produce much energy.

Composite :

Third type of people is composite or the people who are living with both feelings and emotions. Most of us fall under this category. We are normal and calm most of the times, but bounce and raise-voice according to the situation. People belonging to this category have much potential to turn to category 1, that is, people living with feelings; category 2 people have ample opportunities to turn category 3; and category 1 people could become a Yogi or a Sage.

Nolanistic approach in handling feelings and emotions:

If we observe the movies of Chris Nolan, we certainly notice that the characters are mostly living with feelings and they are calm gentlemen dressed up neatly. In Dark Night Trilogy, be it Bruce Wayne or Batman, they never cry. It doesn't mean that they are plain. They have feelings, they love and care for people of Gotham and know how to live happily; Be it Dom Cobb of Inception, he never bursts out though he is full of emotions, but he carries them brilliantly; And how about Will Dormer in Insomnia, played by Al Pacino, can you expect him to cry, he is full of guilt and suffers from insomnia throughout the film, but he is silent and behaves like a nobleman, not easily bursting out; and it is the same with Cooper in Interstellar as well. The whole script of the film is based on the love and affection of Cooper towards his daughter. We also notice similar kind of behavior with Leonard Shelby of Memento, audience feel pity on his condition and he himself knows that he is going through a bad phase of life, but never erupts abnormally. He is calm and carries through his mission.

Now, let's take an example of the master Martin Scorsese's earlier movies, like Mean Streets, Taxidriver, Casino, Good Fellas etc. He is the genius and a living legend of Hollywood. He portrayed the crime and gangsters the best way possible. If we look at his earlier movies, and the impact they created are of course the worst. There are two kinds of audience, those who think and perceive a film as a film and those who take it as real. For the latter kind, Scorsese's movies are dangerous. Those killings while kidding; liberal usage of the word 'fuck' in every dialogue; glorification of the gangsters, volatile characters played by Joe Pesci and his sudden emotional crackups are enough to spoil any young man.

That blood, violence will have a worst impression on certain kind of viewers, these features are used as main theme in the film, and they directly provoke innocent audience to behave in a similar manner. We have to accept this other aspect of the truth as well. Sometimes art is just not for entertainment but a responsible medium for social activism. If we look from this angle, the greatest artist like Scorsese will stand a dwarf as an activist as far as those gangster movies are concerned. But why the world loves Scorsese is his agility and versatility. He intrigues us with thrillers like Shutter Island and Departed, at the same time overwhelms us with an innocent Hugo. If we want to explore the fear in art we can do it in Steven Spielberg way, through a pure creation and art. I feel there is no difference between Jaws and The Duel, both induce fear in every scene but do not provoke spectators for any crime, that's the beauty of art. Sergio Leones western spaghettis are also OK to certain extent, though the violence is portrayed, art dominates the movies and nobody in the streets of New York will imitate a cow boy and ride a horse, but Tommy DeVito of Goodfellas can be imitated every night in any bar by any random guy.

It's agreeable that artist is not meant to be an activist, but that is one aspect of being an artist. Akira Kurosawa did greatest movies of all time and succeeded in upholding the great moral values and propagated the same to all mankind. There is violence in the samurai films like Seven Samurai, Yojimbo, Sanjuro and Ran but the characters are well disciplined, they are woven in such a way that, people should get inspired from them. In Yojimbo the protagonist kills too many people, but the audiences admire him, because of his personality traits and wolf like courageous attitude. It doesn't mean that a director has to be a saint in real life, it's just about the conscience of the director on what he portrays and the quality and quantity of the impact it is going to create on different set of audiences. Roman Polanski was accused of rape, but made few good films and was called a real international director.

When we see these examples, we reasonably conclude that Nolan's feelingly approach is the best. He touches intellectual people with script and narration. Similarly, reaches emotional people with his feelingly characters who don't react suddenly in any tough situations and are full of love and compassion.

It is a subliminal effort of Nolan in making emotional people to behave normal even in difficult circumstances. So the people who belong to category 2&3 are forced in a pleasant way to move towards category 1 invisibly and unconsciously while they watch Nolan's films. When people climb the steps from 3 to 2 or 2 to 1, they become more conscious and start behaving prudently. Thus, the volcano of hatred and anger won't erupt so easily in these men. Instead of reacting suddenly, they will start trying to assess the situation and remain self-controlled. This process reduces deliberate or the willful crimes remarkably. Hence proves the multifaceted talent of sheer genius and a yogi Christopher Nolan.

Three Gunas:

The procedure of elevation from one layer to another is similar to Vedantic idea of YogaSara Upanishad, in which the sages talk about three gunas or the qualities of the mind: Satva, Rajas and Tamas. Satva is purity or light or knowledge, Rajas is activity or love towards the material objects and Tamas is the darkness. So the man full of Satva can easily enter super conscious state. Whereas, man living mostly with Tamas falls in a vicious circle of ignorance. Therefore he has to be raised from Tamas to Rajas and Rajas to Satva. The only possible way to uplift is increasing the satva or being more satvic by the attributes like patience, love, magnanimity, mercy, humbleness, generosity, truthfulness, celibacy etc.

Law of feelings and emotions

Paradigm of law of feelings and emotions:

Feelings	Emotions	Composite of both
Calm and serine	Can burst out anytime with or without external triggers	It depends on the situation
They respond	They react	It can be either of them
Good for the self and society	Not good for self or society	Have the potential to grow to become column 1 i.e. people with feelings
Examples are: Lake, Hydro Power, Minds of Saints	Examples: Ocean, Nuclear Power, Minds of volatile people, Mood swingers (psychologically immature and uncontrolled)	Examples: Rivers, Minds of common people
Buddha, Jesus, Gandhi, Einstein	There are many, but not worth imitating.	Majority of the population
Aware of conscious mind and subconscious	Not aware of conscious mind, dominating subconscious	Aware of conscious mind/may not be aware. Dominating subconscious

It's judicious to know which among these the best is. Since emotions are part of intrinsic nature of human beings, why to dilute them? Why emotions are not good? Because, they just erode the manliness and bring more features of animals. Its wise to understand their respective nature and impacts on an individual and the society.

On the self:

Every small quarrel in the house or neighborhood starts with a reaction. The reaction is not actually a response. Reaction comes out without a filter, it's totally raw, a result of untreated emotions. It's not assessed or analyzed with the help of intellect but an outburst. When the quarrels are multiplied, it leads to a gap, when the gaps are multiplied it leads to breakup. Is breakup good? Is quarrel good? Is reaction good? Is emotion good? One leads to another as it is a chain reaction.

Untreated emotions => Reactions => Arguments/Quarrels /Misunderstandings => Gaps => Breakup We shall see an example, one day Aristotle was sitting at his place and was busy writing something. Few of the villagers went to him and complained 'Your wife is telling some different opinions on you', Aristotle just looked at them and replied 'Well, it is my wife's opinion, you better ask her for more details' and continued his work with a smile on his face.

Now let's place ourselves in the shoes of Aristotle and think what would have been our response. If it's someone psychologically immature, soon after listening to the complaint from the villagers, he might rush to his home and quarrel with his wife. If he is worst, he might go to a bar before heading to house, the quarrel might end up in stabbing, as the man doesn't have control over his actions when he is drunk.

So if you are man of feelings, with Aristotle's attitude, there won't be any clashes, breakups or killings.

On the Society:

If it is true for the self, it is true for the society as well, because society is another term for group of people. If the leaders of a nation are emotionally crude, that country suffers internal as well as external disturbances and may have to face a war. It might look heroic, but many lives are lost. War is glorified by the people who liked it and used it for their self-pride. In reality, anything that kills a human being can never be great. If one man is emotional, he can preach his own methods to others and later to a group. This is how big terrorist groups are formed. They are driven by mere emotions but not the intellect. We have seen the contribution of these people in the relegation of the society.

Our judicial system frames many laws. Every time it encounters a special case, it amends the laws and increases the severity of the punishment for heinous crimes like rape or murder. But do we see any improvement over the course of time or any pleasant results? No! It's going on and on; in fact the number has increased. It's because, nobody thinks about the punishment while committing crime, because they are impaired of thinking. We should look at these issues from a different approach i.e. yogic approach. If we have to eradicate all these crimes, work should be done at the root level and that can be done only through Satsang (gathering together for the truth, being with the truth).Target should be the minds of people. Not the law books.

Emotions are nowhere good, that is the reason Buddhism preaches only feelings. We see all the Buddhist monks cool and composed. Buddha had few willful evil disciples who tried to provoke him, but he never expressed anger or annoyance of their acts. They finally lost for the personality of Buddha.

In order to attain the utmost bliss, we should elevate ourselves to category 1, the person with feelings. It brings a great mental stability that helps us conquer a state of steady wisdom. In Vedanta, there is a beautiful explanation on what is it meant to be a person with mental stability and steady wisdom. Also elucidates how to inculcate such a sublime personality and carry it throughout the life.

Sthitha Prajna:

'Sthitha' means established and 'Prajna' is wisdom. In Bhagavad-Gita (Chapter 2, Verse No.54) Arjuna asks Krishna, who is a Sthithaprajna? what are his properties, how does he talk, how does he sit and how does he walk? In other terms, who is a man of perfection and how does he behave. Lord Krishna replies, He one who is self-contented and firmly established in the self, by renouncing all the desires of the mind is called to be a 'Sthitha Prajna'.

He the one who is neither disturbed by the misery, nor euphoric by the happiness, also free from attachment, fear and anger is called the sage of steady mind. He who is without attachment, who does not rejoice when he obtains good, nor lament when he obtains evil, is firmly fixed in perfect knowledge.

Just like the tortoise drawing back its limbs into its own shell, when a yogi withdraws all the senses from the sense objects, his wisdom is fixed. He is a Sthithaprajna.

Meditation is an attempt to control the mind and concentrate on something temporarily for a certain period of time. Whereas being sthithaprajna is a permanent state of the mind. It is a saadhana (practice) for the seeker and lakshana (property) for the yogi. As we can see from the words of Krishna, a renowned philosopher, sage in Hinduism, sthithaprajna is someone who finds happiness within and doesn't seek it from outside. Instead of being driven by the mind, he uses mind as a medium to illuminate the self and his mind is illuminated by the self. His tranquility is undisturbed by the external causes. When the mind is driven by the sense organs, it is filled with manovikaara's or the mental properties or the disorders like anger, hatred, lust, jealousy and so on, leading to a turbid mind. One cannot lead a blissful life possessing all these disorders in mind. When the water is boiling, we cannot see its depth.

If we witness carefully, the control moves in a bottom up fashion for an ignorant man. All the pain and sorrow is in material world, which is transferred to the mind through senses and hence the mind suffers. The self is obscured and mind is unaware of it.

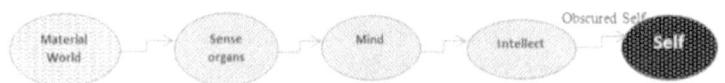

Figure 4.1 Flow of psychic control in case of ignorant man

In the contrary, it should be the reverse. Intellect should drive the mind and mind in turn must control the sense organs. Like the Arjuna sitting in his chariot and regulating five horses! This is the way of sthithaprajna, hence there is question, have you ever wondered why a saint is always happy. A saint is an aspiring sthithaprajna. We are already aware that the self is made up of sachidananda, (Existence, Consciousness and Bliss). Sthithaprajna is established at the self, what he can produce is happiness alone. He is like a divine flower that blossoms and spreads fragrance of happiness unconditionally.

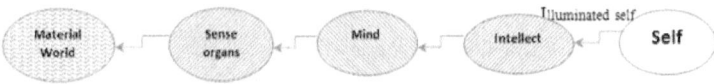

Figure 4.2 Flow of psychic control in case of a SthithaPrajna

One might misinterpret the true motif behind the concept of sthithaprajna. If I don't feel sad when I lose and don't rejoice when I win, where is the motivation for me to achieve something? This question arises in our logical mind, while being in a non sthithaprajna state. But when the mind is tranquil and has achieved this state, it will never remain idle but will engage in more intensive and extra creative work. He with the attitude of sthithaprajna outperforms because he is unworried of the outcome. He accepts it joyously, he is a free bird. His duty is to work, just the way sun shines or the flower blooms and river flows. The nightingale sings better as it is not bothered of any rewards or critics. A sthithaprajna is more intuitive as he bypasses the logical and evaluative mind.

The attitude of sthithaprajna is one of the intrinsic natures of a yogi. It is a great idea to name kids, pets or anything of our favorite as sthithaprajna. This very word itself brings a kind of pleasant feeling and balance in the mind, a peaceful state steals over us. When something is named with such words, people tend to start finding the meaning of it and end up in a mine of diamonds.

How to be a Sthitha Prajna:

The greatest way to achieve this state of mind is very simple, just watch over the mind. It is easy to look out on our thoughts but our true psychological nature is revealed, when we go through a tough situation. For example: When someone tries to do my character assassination by spreading some false rumors about me, how do i respond? Will it be a reaction? When we practice to inspect our thoughts, we certainly analyze them before speaking out. It helps us watch over our behavior during the so called hard circumstances. Many people lost their lives only because of losing control over themselves in such conditions. So how to seek the state of sthithaprajna is to 'just be'. The thoughts and behavior are to be scrutinized, especially in situations where the emotional quotient is challenged. Though we are very well confident and alert on our conscious mind, there is still a chance of emotional eruption because of our subconscious!

Sum total of all the experiences from past thousands of years is stored in our subconscious mind (If we don't believe in rebirth, let's consider it from time of birth). These deep buried tendencies come up into our main mind once in a while. We call them 'Samskaras'. They are formed with likes and dislikes that act as source of emotions. Whenever our main mind encounters something that acts as stimulus to our buried emotions, we might burst out suddenly. When the main mind is free, the thoughts from our subconscious mind are pushed up like bubbles from underneath of lake. Just the way search history is stored in a web browser; thoughts are stacked in subconscious mind. When we type any search term, suggestions start popping up from the history.

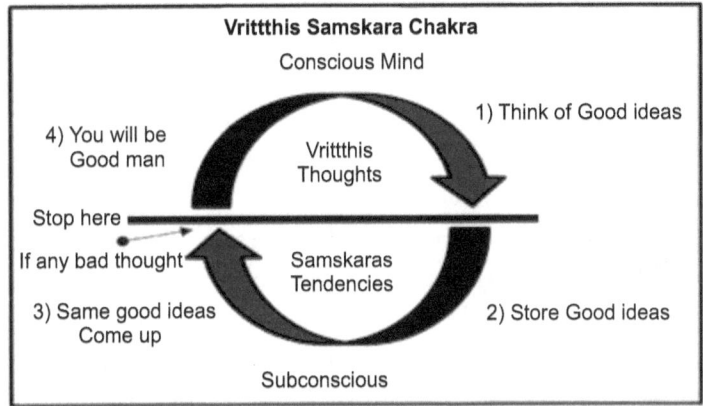

Figure 4.3 *Vritthi Samskara Chakra (Interplay of real-time thoughts and buried tendencies)*

We are incapable to change anything from the subconscious mind, so what must be done? The answer is subconscious itself. The fascinating thing about this circle of subconscious and main mind interaction is, only the recent memories are pushed up to the main mind. So from now on, we have started watching all our thoughts. If they are all good, they get stored on top of the stack of the subconscious mind. So even when they come up, this time they are good thoughts. This is how a man becomes saint. Everyone knows that the status of our present is out of the past and our future will be the result of present. Therefore every small task has a great significance, because it would create an impression on our being. Every small act or the karma contributes to smaskara(tendencies). Our behavior, walk, talk, laughter, even filling a glass of water is going to leave an impression on our being. Therefore with all the awareness, with full of consciousness one should do every task/action more creatively, gracefully and it gradually becomes his/her very nature. This is how the great masters are born just by being vigilant to their thoughts and actions.

One of the prime doctrines discussed constantly in the teachings of Shri J Krishnamurti is, to experience the present moment so intensely that it doesn't create a memory. If it is creating a memory, we are not experiencing the moment in the wholeness. He insisted don't allow the mind to create memories. If we could do that, if no more new memories are being created, just think what happens, the silence builds up in our subconscious. The stack of subconscious will be piled up with the chunks of silence coalescing into one open space of quietness. We will no more be governed by tendencies of subconscious; rather there would be an eternal limbo of silence. There is nothing that comes up like bubbles, because no more bubbles are created. Only the silence echoes within and without the self. All the four blocks of 'vritthi samskara avartha chakra' will have only one common word of 'Silence'. Men who have achieved such state hear the sounds of far off sea and the cosmic music, many people reportedly say, that they see the rainbow when they sit beside an old Buddhist monk. Silence heals, if not today, tomorrow for sure, because silence is the ultimate music.

At this juncture, another important thing to appreciate is, a man with the attitude of Sthithaprajna acquires freedom unknowingly, because freedom is the outcome of a free mind. As a Vedantin, one should be a rebel inside, silence should be his stratagem; we already know that we are not just the body, nor the mind and intellect. Therefore what is there to lose or gain? Dharma should be carried out, after knowing this fact, and then life becomes an interesting game of chess. You are a player and at the same time a spectator. You play the game and become spectator for its results. When you are free from defeat or victory, you are not bound by any laws or the rules of society. If you stand out of these compulsions, you are a free bird.

Now, you will start following your intuition. You will never think, what people will say if you pursue your dream. Or what family members will think about you? Or what will happen if you fail? These all negative thoughts and showstoppers will be wiped out from your way. Once this is done, you will start living. Have you ever seen a free bird sleeping in its nest? It's the nature of free soul to work and do creative things for its self and subsequently it helps the society. That is how things worked from the past unknown.

When your soul is confined with too many laws and rules of the so called society, you just pretend that you are living. You try hard to avoid your dreams or the intuitions because, you will be busy forcing yourself to be mundane and normal like others, to behave just like another white sheep in the herd, because you want to make your parents and yourself proud by being a better and more sophisticated white sheep than others. Do you really need to go through this absurdity at the cost of your dreams? You can be a better creature if you really try to show the guts to leave the herd and listen to your intuition. In order to do that, you have to be a Vedantin. In order to be a Vedantin, you need not wear a robe and wander or subscribe to any religions or dogmas. Just experiment with your mind and try to understand its nature, how it works. That's all.

Now we are aware of why the feelings are good and how to cultivate an attitude of sthithaprajna. It should be clear for us on why there are no wild kisses in Christopher Nolan's films or why there are no dramatic and emotional outbursts. Christopher Nolan succeeds as a filmmaker and wins your heart through his social responsibility as well.

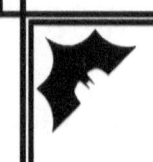 

Fistful of facts about Nolan

- Like a lot of creative people he likes to wear the same outfit every day. In the warmer months this consists of a dark jacket over a blue dress shirt (with slightly fraying collar) and black durable trousers with scuffed, sensible shoes. In the colder months this is paired with a herringbone waistcoat.

- He likes drinking tea so much that he always carries a flask of it around with him, causing his teeth to go a "chestnut gradient".

- Before he begins filming a movie, he spends around two weeks typing out the original idea on his father's old typewriter.

- He doesn't ever like to be too far away from his scripts, so when the actors are reading them he waits in a nearby room.

- He claims that he's never late for work and he never works on weekends.

- He tries to imagine each film he makes as his last, going into it with no compromises.

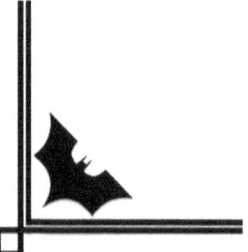 

Chapter 5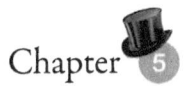

Einstein + Kurosawa

"Truth is more of finding and speculating than settling at it firmly"
-Author

Great Britain has given many great talents to the world of cinema. Few prominent and favorites among them are Alfred Hitchcock, Charlie Chaplin, David Lean, Richard Attenborough and so on. Christopher Nolan is another name to be added into that list in the coming future. It is essential to understand how Chris inherits the qualities of great directors and yet stands unique from them. We can try to grasp the same through a brief glance over selected greats.

Alfred Hitchcock:

Hitchcock is a legend of cinema and one of the auteurs in the art of filmmaking. In a career spanning six decades, he made not less than fifty movies, the best of which are at once suspenseful, captivating, disturbing, funny and romantic. He was widely addressed as 'Master of Suspense' and pioneered many of the techniques in the thriller genre. With his extraordinary command over the film craft, he remains highly influential to this day. Any aspiring filmmaker can skip the dinner but not watching a Hitchcock film. There is so much to learn from every scene and every frame.

His films became popular due to his bold experiments with the human psychology. Irrespective of the plot of the film, suspense and emotions play a key role. Fear, anxiety, phobia, romance are quite common and as he himself said in an interview 'Always make the audience suffer as much as possible', he lived up to his words. For example, in the film Vertigo, the protagonist suffers from acrophobia and the plot itself is based on that. A great suspense can be witnessed in 'Rear Window', at the climax of film when the killer comes closer to the handicapped and unarmed protagonist, audience feel uncomfortable to sit and feel a little handicapped too. The most intriguing and horrific scenes in the movie 'The Birds' and the murder scene in the movie 'Psycho' prove Hitchcock's psychological attack on the audience. Hitchcock proved he is the master of cinema, with his extraordinary sense of composition, lighting and fascinating background score choice. If we observe the climax scene of 'Psycho', where the face of ill mother's corpse is shown, the girl accidentally hits a hanging bulb, that shaking bulb casts a shadow/light effect on the character's face and in turn gets synchronized with the theme music played in background. On the whole it creates a dreadful experience to the audience. 'Strangers on a Train' is a great example of film noir. The character of Bruno, an insane killer with bizarre ideas and absurdist attitude played by Robert Walker, who follows the tennis player everywhere, haunts even the audience.

All great experiments were made and experiences were created when there was nothing digital in the film industry. After these movies, many thrillers were released with more sophisticated sounds and visual effects but they could not deliver what Hitchcock could do. This shows cinema purely needs a third eye of the director to see and experience as the first and foremost viewer while the filming is still in progress.

If we can represent the theme and ingredients of his films in a simple and abstract way, the figure looks like below.

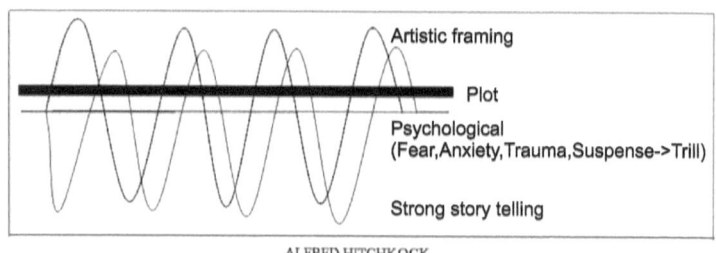

Figure 5.1 Illustration of Alfred Hitchcock's film essence

David Lean:

Sir David Lean made films which are referred to as big screen epics, by using super panvision 70 camera. All the films made by this cinematic genius are path breaking, remarkably great and his later work pretty much redefined what 'Epic' meant. However, his wider filmography reveals an artist of many moods and perfectly capable of indulging them all. What defined Lean and made him the cinematic titan that he will always be was his pure storytelling style and visual grandeur. 'Lawrence of Arabia', 'A bridge on river Kwai' , 'Ryan's Daughter' and 'Passage to India' will remain surely in the list of all-time great movies. If you show a montage from his film to a moviegoer, he would surely identify its Lean's film. His editing work was phenomenal and today it is revered among all film fraternity. One scene is fairly enough to appreciate the master class of David Lean. There is a scene in 'Lawrence of Arabia' to introduce the character of Sherif Ali played by Omar Sharif. It takes two minutes for audience and the other characters to materialize the man on camel. He is dressed in black covered nearly head to toe draws himself out of the mirage in the desert. It creates an unbearable tension when he comes closer as no one knows whether he is a friend or foe until he pulls out a gun and kills guide of Lawrence. The heat of the desert is felt by the audience in this scene, it is one of the most challenging and rewarding scenes in the history of films. Lean had a great conviction to shoot the mirage at any cost. He had said to his cinematographer, 'I don't know how in bloody hell we'll do it, but I want a mirage. Everyone had said that a mirage wouldn't photograph, that it was an illusion of the eye, but one day while on a mudflat I took out my Hasselblad [camera] and there it was, a mirage.'

'Passage to India' is a genuine cinema with extraordinary images capturing India, a land of splendor and paradox. A metaphoric film that depicts cultural, social and political relationship between India and the British. The echoes heard in the Marabar caves reverberate in the trial court too. The film is full of symbolism. Being a British himself Sir Lean, never looks tilted towards the motherland, he made justice as an artist with no boundaries. No other director could have accomplished the task of adapting E.M Forster's Novel to motion pictures with such excellence as Sir Lean did.

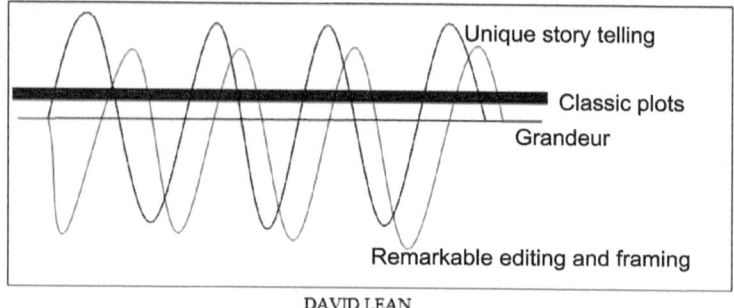

Figure 5.2 Illustration of David Lean's film essence

Martin Scorsese and Steven Spielberg:

If we reflect upon contemporary American cinema, two main pillars are to be considered: Martin Scorsese and Steven Spielberg. We could also see Coppola and Lucas, but however based on versatility and works, former two could be visited. Scorsese is an exceptional director who can create an essence of hypnotism and hangover in his films. Once you watch the complete movie and come out, you will have a true and core aftereffect of it for few days. When you watch his most magnetic film 'Taxi Driver', the narration and loneliness of Travis will stay with you for long. Those dim lights and New York streets, eerie background music will haunt you. It is the same with his other gangster flick 'Good Fellas' and a psychological thriller 'Shutter Island'. No other director on earth could portray the gangsters and crime as Scorsese did. Scorsese's cinematic genius is so unique that, he made classics out of blood and violence. One of the Scorsese's underrated film 'After Hours' guarantees that most of the viewers will have night mares after watching it.

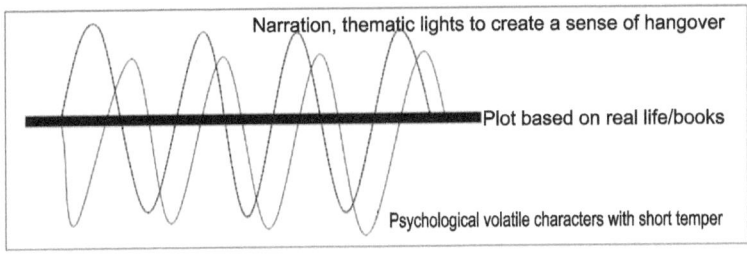

Figure 5.3 Illustration of Martin Scorsese's film essence

In the contrary Steven Spielberg is a pure creator and a visionary. In the beginning of his career he made intriguing horror films like 'Duel' and 'Jaws' that gave a totally new and unusual experience to the audience. And then came, 'Close Encounters of Third Kind' and 'Extra Terrestrial' that changed the movies forever. Spielberg made impossible possible with his films 'Jurassic park' and 'Artificial Intelligence'. He got well versed in creation and presentation of the same in a sumptuous way. He succeeds in converting even adult audience into a child and then astonishes them with sounds and spectacle. He exhausted all genres of the cinema and won Academy award for a wartime cult classic 'Schindler's List'. At his 70s he is still the most active director in Hollywood and has a pipeline of projects.

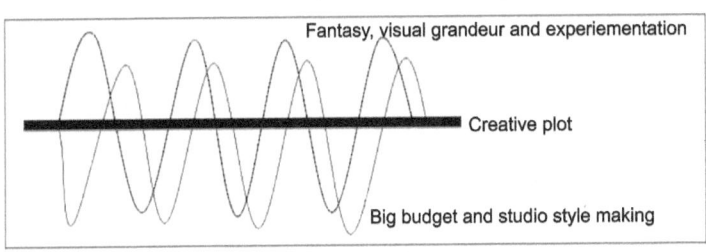

Figure 5.4 Illustration of Steven Spielberg's film essence

Akira Kurosawa:

If we glance through all the surveys and rankings of all-time favorite directors, a common name appears on top in all of the lists, Akira Kurosawa, one of the stalwart directors in the history of cinema. There is no filmmaker who is unaware of Kurosawa. He is one of the pioneers to introduce the cinema of Japan to the world in a large scale. All the veterans in the field of cinema like Ingmar Bergman, Satyajit Ray, Fellini loved and praised Kurosawa's work. Through his excellent craftsmanship in the art and auteur persona, he managed to create a great impact on other filmmakers be it western or eastern. Kurosawa was a highly disciplined technician; he meticulously reviewed every shot and worked frame by frame. He came into limelight at international level after the 'Rashomon's victory in Venice film festival. Hollywood says, all filmmakers have one or two masterpieces, but Kurosawa holds six to eight in his name. He created many characters that are self-questioning and retrospective that helped audience to connect easily and be in the character's shoes and enjoy the film. Kurosawa's approach was pure and genuine art with full of morality and mature characters with noble attitude. His vision could be understood by the films like Seven Samurai, Rashomon, Ran, Ikiru, Scandal, Yojimbo, Sanjuro etc. The movie 'Ikiru' is an eye-opener to the modern man, where everyone leads more of a mechanical life without any creativity or basic awareness of what and why. It would serve its purpose even if it is released today, because the subject director chose is not bound by the time and it portrays the meaning of life in 2 hours. Movie indirectly conveys, you try to find the meaning of life, only when you confront the death! But it is too late to live!. It doesn't mean, Kurosawa did only movies of moral elements but he took up war movies like 'Seven Samurai' and 'Ran'; same way psychological and intellectual thriller 'Rashomon'; and the pure art like 'Dreams'. Kurosawa's movies have become a syllabus for the film students, because of their standards and sophistication in terms of scene composition, lighting, editing and symbolic approach. To give an example, there is a scene in the movie 'Ikiru'. The protagonist has lead the life full of misery, though he is a government servant, unhappy with his profession, resigns from the work after learning that he has cancer and about to die in another six months. Wandering in the quest of happiness, he eagerly wants to find solace before he dies. One day a young girl, who worked as his subordinate, reveals the secret of happiness to him with her toy. Her happiness is to make toys for children, so she takes chance in life by resigning to her government job! She says "Making them, I feel like playing with every baby in Japan" moved by her wisdom, protagonist walks down the stairs in delight from the restaurant holding the rabbit toy in his hand, at the same time there is a birthday party going on at the other side of the restaurant. When the hero comes down, all the kids start singing 'Happy birth day to you' to the birthday girl, but that moment creates a magic in the audience and the hero because, it looks like as though they sang for him and he really starts living from that very day. Such symbolism is in abundance in the films of Kurosawa. Every scene in the movie, 'Seven Samurai' is worth mentioning and that's the reason it stands as the real masterpiece till date.

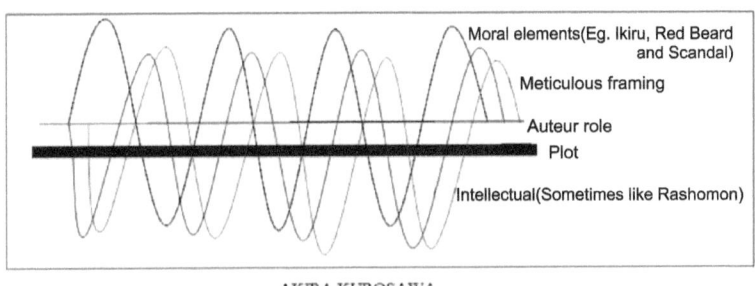

Figure 5.5 Illustration of Akira Kurosawa's film essence

Satyajit Ray:

A pioneer of parallel cinema in India, Satyajit Ray began his film journey through a classic craft of art 'Pather Panchali'(song of the road). He was known for his auteur persona. Right from the script, Ray involved in every aspect of filmmaking, he even composed music whenever music directors were unavailable. Ray designed poster himself for all of his films and involved in editing as well. He also handled the camera partially during his initial days. When Ray did 'Chess Players', Sir Richard Attenborough played one of the characters in the movie. Talking about the all-inclusive nature of Ray he says 'He writes the screenplay, he composes the music, he directs it, he operates the camera. He half-lights the set. Certainly he works with the lighting cameraman in such detail that any source of light or change that he wants he gets. He edits his own films, almost as Chaplin did'. Mr. Ray has written many short story collections, made illustrations and it is surprising to know that the Plaque awarded for the Sahitya Akademi winners(literary honor by the national academy of letters, India) is designed by Ray.

Ray was inspired by Hollywood films and he inspired back as well, Martin Scorsese has said in many occasions that Ray was one of his inspirations. When the filmmaker involves in every phase and facet of cinema, he gets a collective comprehensive capability that will give him a wider picture of the film. And such films will have the signature of the director in every aspect, it becomes more apparent as the work excels. It's interesting to see the academy note, when Ray was honored with academy award for lifetime achievement. The note says *"In recognition of his rare mastery of the art of motion pictures, and of his profound humanitarian outlook, which has had an indelible influence on filmmakers and audiences throughout the world."*

Stanley Kubrick:

Though all the directors have their own style of approach and making, there is one director who is an exception. It's Stanley Kubrick, a synonym for experimentation. He was a genuine talent of Hollywood and who was obsessed with the art of cinema. Kubrick experimented in every facet of filmmaking, from the camera angles to the very subject that he chose. If we observe other directors, there is a kind of consistency and a stereotype. In the contrary, Kubrick doesn't belong to that league. If we see '2001: A space Odyssey' and then the "A clockwork orange" one might find it hard to believe that both of these films are directed by the same person. Former is a benchmark cinema in the Hollywood and pioneer in the space adventure films, whereas latter looks like a Sequel of Scorsese's 'Mean Streets', saying metaphoric or the satiric. Kubrick made justice to whatever the concept that he chose to 100%. No other director on earth would have made 'The Shining' the way it is now; its extraordinary filming and his signature low angle shots made this movie a classic cinema.

After the release of 'Interstellar', many people started comparing Chris Nolan with Kubrick. However both of these greats are unique and different in their own style. Both are similar in case of vigor to challenge and push themselves; attitude to do something beyond and something that's not done in the past. Nolan is experimental too but there is a consistency in whatever film he makes. Consistency is great and inconsistency is greater when it comes to films. Hence there is no point in comparing these greats but to appreciate their dedication and contribution to the art of cinema.

Now, if we note the films made by Chris Nolan, in this context, we can see all of these elements seen above are inherited in his films. Hitchcock's psychology(Like that of Memento and Insomnia) and visual story telling(repeatedly showing a particular object to give clues and close up shots with the objects of importance) ; Kurosawa's morality and genuine art ; Spielberg's creativity(Nolan created a completely different world of dreams through Inception); Scorsese's cinematic hypnotism and hangover(for example, Memento gives the same effect as that of Taxi Driver, the narration and background music and the POV leaves audience in a same kind of aftereffect); Stanley Kubrick's experimentation (space adventure after the heist thriller); David Lean's grandeur (In terms of using Panvision /IMAX camera too) and so on.

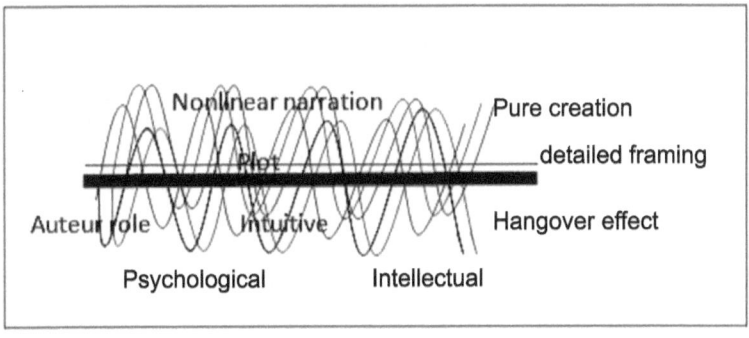

Figure 5.6 Illustration of Christopher Nolan's film essence

There are directors who are favorites only among the filmmakers. They have a great name in the film fraternity due to their technical excellence in filmmaking and there are few who are favorites of audience and rest are pets of critics. Nolan is liked by all three categories of the people. His extraordinary skills in craft, brilliant way of presentation and the blend of both technicality and the mass appeal make him a true genius of cinema. He holds one imaginary thread in his fictional plot and tries to question the truth putting a hand on the shoulder of the audience. This very character of challenging himself along with the audience marks Nolan as one of the most engaging directors of our time.

Science and Intuition:

Science was born when man started observing the nature and tried to understand its laws and features. When you go deeper into any field of it, you become specialized in it. There are certain streams in science that have boundaries and fixed rules, there are specializations that obey your reasoning, for example: in biology, human anatomy is same for all the doctors in the world, cells are similar for everyone, we are developing enhanced apparatus and medicines to cure a disease but whatever that you study in medicine is about the body and within the body but not beyond it. In this sense, this field of science is limited, whereas cosmology and theoretical physics are as vast and unbound as the universe itself. They are a different worlds of study all together.

Intellect is used to perceive the things, apply reasoning and deduce an equation in order to produce an output. It becomes silent when it encounters countless stars in the sky. You need something beyond the intellect to deal with this subject i.e. Intuition. Many scholars can reckon on something which is light years away by the calculations, facts and figures that they have on table. But there are cases where those facts and figures do not hold good anymore! And sometimes they are proven completely wrong after certain extent of time. There is speculation on the plausibility of the theories every day. If x is 1 today it can become 10 or 0 anytime. Initially we had assumed that man was the center of universe and later we realized we are just a part of a galaxy in the huge universe. Then the universe was thought to be static, after that it's proved to be expanding, then the nature of the stars, neutron stars, black holes, wormholes and so on. We are yet to find, is it the only universe or there are many? Is it only made up of matter and energy or does it possess something more? What is the nature of dark energy? We see this world, is it because we are made up of matter and energy? What was there before the Big Bang? Can we simulate event horizon? What happens if the Big Bang is reversed from now? If the energy is spread all over the universe, is our consciousness a form of energy? Is it transformed from the energy? And so on.

The reasoning gets handicapped after certain range, further journey needs pure intuition, a divinely language that speaks from within, just have to listen to it and move forward. Cosmology needs that Intuition. It is very rare and very few people are blessed with it. Albert Einstein was one of them.

Theoretical physicist should be a philosopher before becoming a scientist, in order to approach the truth and make assertions through intuition. He should also have that affectionate and loving heart towards humanity. We are aware that Einstein was influenced by Friedrich Nietzsche and Schopenhauer's ideas. He was the rarest of men who really tried to find the truth about existence both through inner and the outer science along with spreading peace and harmony in the world. Einstein also prioritized Intuition over the reasoning mind. As he says, *"The intuitive mind is a sacred gift and the rational mind is a faithful servant. We have created a society that honors the servant and has forgotten the gift."*

Let's take an example, what is beauty? Is there something called beauty exists? In a scenario where our mind accepts a fair skinned lady with straight nose and red lips with neat eyes as beautiful. Why the black is not beautiful? Our mind is prejudiced, as and when it sees, it perceives and begins comparison of those properties with a predefined set of ideas stored in the past.

We can try to understand the intuitive mind and the rational mind with an example, if we assume that, a director has to make a film on flower, The Jasmine. The intuitive mind feels the beauty of jasmine, without any mediate like mind, and might give some insight or the truth and the aesthetic experience about the flower immediately. Whereas the rational mind, perceives it and then compares its petals with other flowers like rose and studies the colors of it with all the existing information. Subsequently concludes it after a great research that, jasmine is a small flower, it has no variety of colors, but has a great fragrance etc.

Here both of the views are acceptable because both are true in nature, latter is more common and every mind possesses this property, however intuition is rare and very few possess that gift. But it should not be misunderstood for some superstitious omens or the blind hope in something. For example, there is a Cricket match going on between England and Australia. Assume that I am pro Britain and I am betting 100$. It is final over, only 2 balls are left and English team needs 18 runs to win. My mind doesn't want to lose 100$ so it goes for a blind hope, though I know England will lose the match, I will say 'we will win, my intuition says so'. It's just the false hope that gives us some comfort. Hence we should be logical and rational in every possible way without any compromises, at the same time we should be free of prejudices.

Many of us think that the intuition comes by birth, but all monks of Buddha order say it can be cultivated. Buddha was the most logical and rational man. He said, 'Don't believe in anything until you experience it on your own'. At the same time they say, empty your mind to listen to your intuition. A popular Zen monk Shunryu Suzuki says, *'If your mind is empty, it is always ready for anything, it is open to everything'*. It is when we clear off the ripples in mind and settle it calmly; we can see the depth clearly. A great poet Khalil

Gibran says, *"When you reach the end of what you should know, you will be at the beginning of what you should sense."* We should expand our souls to feel for the universe. Intuition flows through them who are in a rhythm with the soul of universe.

If we notice accomplished men like Albert Einstein, Nikola Tesla, Galileo or our recent favorite Steve Jobs, we notice that the intuition worked for them, and we also are aware about the facts that they preferred solitude. Albert Einstein used to sail on a small yacht with a pen and a paper. Tesla had no friends. Knowingly or unknowingly, they all prepared their mind for Intuition. They heard from the soul of universe, the music of eternity. When the channel of mind becomes clear, Brahman speaks through it and reveals his secrets.

Same way when it comes to Chris Nolan, he is not into social networking or doesn't even use a cellphone as per reliable sources around him. It's evident that he wants to remain in solitude; it may not be a physical but a mental solitude. He wants time to frame thoughts in his mind. It's possible only when your mind is empty. There is enormous amount of garbage rolling through the social media every single minute, he doesn't want to waste his life by following or going through it. This way his mind remains unaffected and unadulterated. It shows that the secret of extraordinary men is intuition and it comes when you dump all the trash of the mind and open up to the inner voice. For the synthetic vision and the reconciling view, we have to transcend intellect by means of intuition. A film like Interstellar could be made only if you are blessed with such intuition. Christopher Nolan worked with great theoretical physicist Kip Thorne for this film. While explaining the science of interstellar in his book, Kip Thorne writes, 'As we talked, it became clear that Chris knew a remarkable amount of relevant science and had deep intuition about it. His intuition was occasionally off the mark, but usually right on. And he was tremendously curious.' Interstellar is a perfect blend of Science, Art and Philosophy; all three of them go well and end up in sublimity, only if you have a great intuition. If we try to understand them separately, it won't make much sense as they are meant to be together. It will be a foolish idea to understand them discretely, but becoming foolish is also interesting because you become someone else knowingly with all awareness. It's just like saying, 'I am thinking that, I am thinking'. When it comes to science, film teaches basics of cosmology and physics to the laymen brilliantly with much ease. The theory of relativity, gravity, wormhole, blackhole, Newton's third law etc. (even the botany! with blight)

Core theme of philosophy in the film is, only human beings can save themselves and no one else. Only "THEY" can uplift themselves : It is very interesting that in the beginning, when they speak of 'They' , the advanced civilization , who can view the time as a physical dimension, audience think that it should be some aliens but in the climax its revealed that its 'We'.

When Cooper falls into Gargantua blackhole, he slips into a tesseract built by bulk beings through which he sends signals to his daughter Murph. When Professor Stephen Hawking talks about the blackholes in his book 'Theory of Everything', he beautifully explains it with the example of astronaut and his spaceship rotating the blackhole exactly the way envisioned by Christopher Nolan. In the lecture he says, astronaut falling into a blackhole won't be saved by god and can't go back in time and change the past (and also Kip Thorne states it as 'dubious') however Nolan has made a great idea to hold both of these ideas good. It is the same Cooper who sent signals through gravity anomalies and who shook the hand with Brand while she passed through the wormhole, this very idea gives the whole movie a new dimension, the circular/infinite time. This is where we should bow down to Christopher Nolan. It's our descendants who save us and we are our own saviors.

How the man is helpless and slave of time, its irony that the Murph is old and on deathbed when Cooper is still in his 50s. : This element makes us think that death is really needed and it's a provocative fact for us to escape it (Death is just like Tiger in the movie Life of Pie). How to escape? What is death? How it comes? We are bound by the time, our body ages out, so we die. What if we can escape time and go into the realm of infinity, where there is no death or birth! If we have to go there, we need to understand what time is. It is a subject of both science and philosophy. The issue with time teaches us both the theory of relativity and the misery of man. Death is necessary, because only death can keep man alive.

Love can transcend the dimensions; gravity could be understood and measured but not the love. There is no Chandrashekhar's limit for love. The real glory of the movie is, all the complex theories, laws and problems are inclusive in one grand story of a relation between the father and daughter. Just the way movie begins, audience are soothed and made familiar to the plot with intricate relationship of Cooper and his daughter Murph. It will be there in the mind of audience throughout the film till the last scene, where we see a sophisticated Cooper station that orbits Saturn. And Murph is on death bed, brings tears in audience eyes when she utters *'Because my Dad had promised me'* about the surety on Cooper's coming back.

Christopher Nolan says indirectly that, there are many things that we don't understand. We just have to feel them. There is also some moral philosophy in the film, like Dr. Mann's self-goal teaches us be good do good. In a whole, a documentary type material is made a great motion picture; with all the essence of art and commercial elements, including both science and fiction. It wouldn't have been possible without Christopher Nolan and his intuition.

It is the same universal consciousness that manifests as chunks through different individuals. Therefore there is no surprise, it just tries to reveal itself through human mind, and we call it with different names like art, science or philosophy. We are just the channels for its mysterious flow, need to purify and remove all debris from the mind.

So that it can flow free and easy. Kurosawa says *'Man is a genius when he is dreaming'*, Christopher Nolan made people genius through his dreams. What else the humanity could expect from art or science. Let's hope to witness a civilization that is more sublime and sophisticated than the Atlantis. Where people live with full of intuition, where there is no place for the issues like communal extremism, racism, regionalism etc. Let the love be another dimension and the truth the way of life. The life of bulk beings!

Fistful of facts about Inception

- If you take the first letter of the main characters Dom, Robert, Eames, Arthur, Mal and Saito you get DREAMS.

- Ariadne's hair is in a tight bun in the hotel sequence so filmmakers didn't have to figure out how her hair should move in zero-gravity.

- When Cobb gave Ariadne the puzzle test, Ariadne's final solution was a diagram of King Minos' Labyrinth. Ariadne is the name of King Minos' daughter in the same mythology.

- A series of numbers keeps appearing: the number that Fischer gives Cobb/Arthur is 528491, The two hotel rooms used are rooms 528 and 491, the number that Eames (as a woman) gives to Fischer is 528-491, the combination to the strong room starts with 52, and the combination to the safe is 528-491. This is all to reinforce the importance of the number throughout the film.

- In the city scene on the first level of the dream with Fischer, the state motto on the license plates of the cars reads "The Alternate State."

Chapter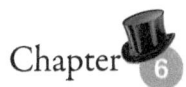

When I interviewed Nolan

It was the most delightful moment of my life. I had never imagined that, one day I would sit with Christopher Nolan and talk of cinema and philosophy. The room was all dark and there was a three point lighting setup. Once the tall man in suits arrived, I started feeling the same vibrations as that of a remote cave in far distant Himalayas. I could feel those hidden ethos of the renaissance period and heard the echoes from deep down well of batman. I felt he is from the world of Atlantis.

I shook his hand and greeted "Hello Sir!" Chris gave a mysterious smile and settled down on his seat. He looked like an enlightened yogi to me, with that innocent yet gleeful smile. I was given a less time to talk to a timeless man, so I began with my first question about Indian cinema.

✦ **Sir what's your view on Indian films and filmmakers?**

Well, having a rich heritage of art, India is multicultural and you cannot evaluate films made there. I would say they are making very entertaining and good films. Filmmakers there are free to make any kind of film's they want, as there are no obligations or any specific demands from the audience.

✦ **You are being more diplomatic!? Why can't Indian filmmakers do intellectual films like you do?**

It totally depends on the perception. I make films to render entertainment and certain classes of audiences call it intellectual. May be it's the same case with Indian films and filmmakers.

✦ Why can't we make an inception in India?

Hahaha(he laughs with that regular mischievous look) you got to ask them, every filmmaker wants to tell a story that are relevant to their targeted audience. Great films are made when there are great audiences. Big studios should come forward with all guts and encourage original ideas and new scripts.

If you say audience are not competent enough to digest such films, should uplift the minds of audience. If you say audiences are downgraded, it's only because of the film's that are made. If you want to uplift, it's only through the films again.

✦ How could you write great witty dialogues in your films?

I am from literature background, what I write is just apt to the character. I weigh and check the psychological depth and background of the character then try to make justice to it.

[I realized that Chris had answered all of my questions related to cinema in his other interviews. Instead of that, I thought to switch to the philosophy soon, which is like other hidden surface of the moon].

✦ Chris, somewhere you said that, "Chase your reality!" When the whole world is busy chasing dreams.

Yeah I said it with respect to the climax scene of Inception, but perhaps it's very true, We are living in our own subjective reality and we never know whether what we see is real or not or does this universe exists in the absence of us. This very existence looks like a grand long dream for me. We might understand it well on the day, this so called reality and the dreams become one.

✦ Which do you think is the reality?

I don't think we can objectify something and call it a reality. But I feel there is a common and universal truth that we all are seeking for and there is no way to get to it until we escape our subjective reality.

For example, we think dream as our reality while dreaming and we think this wakeful state is our reality now. Hahaha it's a helpless state of a human being, but one thing is common between both of these versions, the watcher, the witness. If a tiger chases me in a dream, I just run away and at the same time I am witnessing that I am running. In wakeful state, I might climb a tree or something. It's just the level of consciousness is different in these versions and witness is the same.

✦ We are so small in this vast universe and could not even cross our solar system, don't you think our space missions to find an inhabitable planet is going futile?

Its just a part of evolution, the evolution stops when the struggle ends. We might build a colony in other planet soon or at least the next generations, but it is true that we cannot go on traversing planet by planet in this vast and expanding universe. We need to incorporate another method of seeking reality. Everybody agrees that universe is made up of matter and energy and nothing else. Our body is matter and the consciousness is energy, but we need to try little harder to find out the true nature of this consciousness. If we can simulate the mind and consciousness, we can compete with the creator or the god!

✦ Why are you suspicious about the reality of this world?

The Change!. Whatever that changes is not permanent. And whatever that's not permanent cannot be real. Very simple!. You might say, our mind is also changing. Yes! Our mind is continuously changing and that's why it's not real. If you observe closely, if you do not have any thoughts for a moment, there is no explicit existence for the mind. There is nothing as such called mind in the absence of thoughts.

Many of our theoretical physicists are saying the universe is continuously expanding, so it's changing and when it's changing it's not permanent, so it's not real!

✦ **How can you be so sure, that there is something constant beyond this changing phenomenon?**

Well, as I said earlier, this entire universe is made up of two things, matter and force/energy, even the human being. Sometimes I feel humans are but miniature versions of the nature. We are also made up of matter and energy. There is something that governs both of these in us, as well as the entire universe. That governor of these is constant and unchanging. For example, in the states of dream and wakefulness, witness is the constant. It's the same way. I know that I am in my body and I do not need any mediate organs to prove my own existence. Its intuition or the immediate perception of the self. No philosophers or scientists are needed to prove the existence of the self. It's implicit. Self is just the spectator of everything. This world is an object for him.

✦ **What is time according to you? Can anybody escape it?**

Time is relative experience to the mind. Its blend with our mind and creates a feeling of past, present and the future. If anything that changes, it is bound by the time. For example, all this material existence is aging out. It is bound by the time and it is in time. If there is something that never changes, then it is not in time. The only timeless existence is 'The self' and is already beyond the time, so one need not escape as he is already outside the realm of it.

✦ **People tend to believe that you have chosen cinema as a medium to propagate your ideas and philosophy, is it true?**

No, I make films to entertain, but it's good that people find philosophy in them. And I liked films because it is a different world altogether and you can create anything that you want here. Whatever you imagine can be painted on screen, you always have opportunities to do something different every time. It's a kind of thrill and amusement. I challenge myself and I just think, what kind of a movie that I want to see if I am the audience, so I make one. I respect the money and time of audience. I want to show something that they have never seen or experienced before.

✦ Is it the books or films that impact more on our lives?

Both of these mediums have certain impacts but the degree of it varies. I say books have deeper impact than films. When you read it, you will create your own version of a motion picture in your mind. And you have ample time to comprehend and digest. Your mind will be running behind the lines and you can pause in between to have a glimpse of some insights that come only after a deep sip of a thought. Whereas films are lively and they won't wait for you, here both are running together, your mind and the movie. You can't pause and think, what you will have is a different state of mind after you come out from theatre. There is more of knowledge in the books and films offer experience. I would say, film is more powerful medium than books and you reach masses of all kinds.

✦ In Dark Knight Trilogy you portrayed moral ambiguity and crime. What is your solution for unstoppable crime in modern world?

I am an artist but not an activist, but in my opinion on curbing the crime, is to make people think, to help them evolve psychologically and intellectually. Only weak minded perform such activities, only they are prone to bad habits and addictions. Be it Joker or Bane, there were no one to educate them. They believed destruction is their birth right; there were no one to uplift their minds, so the result.

Crime is a spontaneous action. It occurs when emotions dominate over intellect. If you channel your emotions towards positive things like art and science, there won't be a crime. Political laws are just cure but not the prevention. If we have to work at root level, then it's just by educating people, helping them evolve and provide a pleasant environment to grow up.

Here, one more aspect is, most of us have identified ourselves with the mind. We are not matured enough to see mind as just an internal organ. We say, 'I am depressed', 'I am devastated', 'I don't like him/her'. It is mind that doesn't like and it is mind that is feeling low. Not the 'I'. We should learn to stand away from the mind and try to observe and analyze why it behaves that way. Peaceful mind never disturbs anything in this world.

✦ **Why your films do not contain romance or a beautiful couple with happy relationship?**

Characters are woven according to the story, and if you observe, most of my film plots revolve around relationships. Be it Memento, Inception or even the Interstellar. Beauty and the happiness are totally different aspects and we cannot relate them. We cannot guarantee happiness wherever there is beauty, in the materialistic world. Its only love that keeps every relationship alive, happiness and beauty in the heart automatically follow where there is love. Love is the key for both.

✦ **What is the meaning of beauty and happiness according to you?**

Haha, How can I say the meaning of it? If something has a meaning, then it cannot be beauty. Beauty is something that bypasses evaluating mind. If there is something beautiful, you can just feel it. You really can't understand it. It's your immediate perception. If you are able to understand it, it's not beauty anymore.

And the second part of your question, happiness. It is the pursuit of all the creatures on this planet. According to me, it is just an unconditional state of the mind. But where we fail is, we condition it with many things. We say, I will be happy only if I become a millionaire, or only if I visit Paris, or only if I marry the girl I want etc. And once we achieve it, it's the same mind with some temporary joy, again we set ourselves a goal for it. If we condition it for something, it cannot last. So it should be unconditional. Prison or the palace, be happy. But when you are capable enough to live in a palace, why choose a prison? Just play your game, what you gonna lose ultimately.

✧ **Chris, you lived an American dream too and made fortune.**

Yes! But I was happy even while making indie films. My happiness doesn't depend upon my profession or whatsoever.

✧ **Then what is the goal of this life?**

Being happy forever is the goal of life. When I say forever, It means everlasting. But what we are doing is, we are trying to find happiness in the things that are not permanent but temporary. We set goals to ourselves like, if I build a house or buy a car or become an engineer in NASA, then I will be happy. And after few days of achieving it, they won't give me happiness, because everything is changing including mind. So, that kind of happiness won't last forever.

If we cling to something that is permanent then only we can get permanent happiness. If anything that is permanent in this universe, is only the 'Self'. So we need to get rid of the changing world and mind. And embrace the never changing self by self. In simple terms, we pour water into a bottle and convince ourselves that, shape of the water is bottle. Such mentality will never give us happiness. We should try to understand the actual shape of the water, without any bottles or the jars.

✧ **That's a kind of deep philosophy! How do you decide upon a concept, How do you think?**

For me, thinking is a process of becoming one with the thought. There is no separation between thinker and the thought, because they cannot exist independently. When I think of something, I am completely invested in it and I myself do not drive any thought but the thought drives itself along with me. When there is a new thought, there is an immense opportunity to portray it many ways. One truth can be told in many different ways. I just try to find attractive way and the thought should be fascinating which can challenge me and the audience.

If the gravity of the idea is strong enough, it directs you through the entire process of making it into a film.

The table started shaking, the glasses sliding off the table; the hanging light started behaving a pendulum; there is an immense strangeness in the place; there is a shift of gravity; the weather started turning anomalous; the roof started collapsing in the corner; a very familiar but an unknown feeling, I hear a perplexing music. I started shivering, Nolan smiled and walked away. The roof top collapsed over my head and I am dead.

I woke up, tried to control my breath. It was 3AM, I was all alone in my room perplexed!, drank some water, looked outside the window. It was drizzling, a dog was barking, a guy with a trolley is walking alone in the street under yellow mercury light, the road is all golden colored and shining. May be he landed from a late-night flight. I tried to take out my camera and click him. But I felt I just don't want to repeat a 'Rear Window' of Hitchcock. Closed my window gently and glanced at Nolan's poster on the wall and slept. What a scary and thrilling dream it was!

Fistful of facts about Inception

- Marion Cotillard's character is called 'Mal', short for name 'Malorie', a name derived from French word 'malheur', meaning misfortune or unhappiness. The shorter version 'mal' means wrong/bad or evil (when a noun) in French, as well as some other Latin-based languages.

- In an effort to combat confusion, television broadcasts in Japan included text in the upper-left corner of the screen to remind viewers which level of the dream a specific scene takes place in.

- The running time of 2 hours 28 min is a reference to the original length of Edith Piaf's song "Non, je ne regrette rien", which lasts (on its first recorded edition) 2 minutes 28 seconds

- The name of the character Cobb references Henry N. Cobb, an American architect notable for designing skyscrapers. The world Cobb and Mal made in Limbo consists mostly of skyscrapers. And also the name of thief from his first film 'Following'

- There is a series of numbers that keep appearing, on the front of the train the number is 3502, the taxi number is 2305 and the hotel room number is 5302.

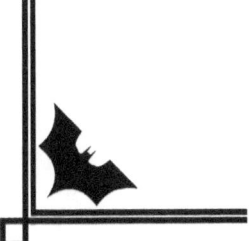

104

Chapter 7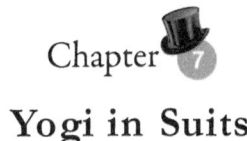

Yogi in Suits

tapasvibhyo dhiko yogi
jnanibhyo pi mato dhikah
karmibhyas cadhiko yogi
tasmad yogi bhavarjuna
Bhagavadgita (chapter 6, Sankhyayoga verse 46)

"A yogi is greater than the ascetic, greater than the empiricist and greater than the fruitive worker; Therefore, O Arjuna, in all circumstances, be a yogi."

Yoga :

It is essential to understand the spirit of 'Yoga' before trying to comprehend a 'Yogi'. In the language of gods Sanskrit, the word Yoga comes from the root 'yuj', which means, to attach or to unite. It is a method to synchronize the body and the mind, in order to unite or become one with the existence. It has many connotations that are to be used based on the contexts like, to yoke, concentration, and harness etc.

In our times, yoga refers to a physical exercise and more of a business in the east and west. Twisting and twining body alone could never be called as yoga, it's merely circus. According to Patanjali Maharshi, an eminent master, who laid foundation for the classical Yoga Philosophy through his work '*Yoga Sutras*', Yoga in one sentence is, "*yogaschitta vritthi nirodah*" that means 'Yoga is removal of fluctuations of the mind'. It's like subduing the waves over the surface of a pond that distorts our view of bottom. In other words, its bringing our mind into an utter tranquility, so that one experiences the life as it is without any misconceptions, for example, a) If we are occupied with some work, we think time is moving faster, here the world is same and time also is normal, but we experience and perceive it differently because our mind is engaged in something relentlessly. b) When we see smoke from a distance, we come to a conclusion that there must be fire. Smoke could have been caused because of any other reason too. c) Based on his attire we decide the profession of a man. d) Since we are used to a beginning and end for everything, like a movie, a book, our life span etc. We tend to think that universe also has a beginning and an end or the time has a start and an end etc. When we come over all the prejudices, we see the things in their true nature. Yoga is all about that.

For a raw mind, there is a danger that the perception can be colored with the presumptions. Natural maladies of the mind like hatred, jealousy, anger can lead to more misunderstandings and consequences which take us away from the truth. If our mind is conditioned from the childhood that dark is ugly and white is beautiful, our mind continues to perceive the same. Whenever we see anything dark, there is already a preconception in our mind about darkness, therefore that perception cannot give us truth. If we perform any action in anger, there is a chance of failure or damage. If we shake hand of our friend with full of jealousy in the mind, how could our wish originate from the heart and how can it reach his/her heart. To see an apple as an apple mind should be clean and crystal. Then there will be a direct experience of everything.

Many of the scholars, who are overburdened with collected information or knowledge, are likely to miss the experience. It is a worst kind of presumption in the mind. For example: When you read, that god is infinite consciousness and eternal bliss, that belief system is created in the mind. It may turn perilous for a seeker, as he might stop his seeking at this point. There is no point in reading and remembering god is infinite consciousness. One should try hard to comprehend and experience it. What is infinite? What is consciousness? What is infinite consciousness? All spiritual masters say, *be quiet, be alert, be quietly alert, be alertly quiet*. The mind of the scholars will just appreciate these lines and go further to read next. If someone can practice it even for one day, he/she will get enlightened same day. Therefore, yoga has got nothing to do with the knowledge but with experience. Yoga is all about eradicating all these misconceptions and flux of the mind to have a direct or immediate experience of the existence and to become one with it.

Yogi :

In simple terms, yogi is the one who practices yoga. One of the greatest Yogis of all time, Paramahamsa Yogananda in his autobiography, while illuminating on the difference between a swami (monk) and a yogi, says "Anyone who practices a scientific technique of God-contact is a yogi; he may be either married or unmarried, either a worldly man or one of formal religious ties. A swami may conceivably follow only the path of dry reasoning, of cold renunciation; but a yogi engages himself in a definite, step-by-step procedure by which the body and mind are disciplined, and the soul liberated. Taking nothing for granted on emotional grounds, or by faith, a yogi practices a thoroughly tested series of exercises which were first mapped out by the early rishis"

Likewise we can get many annotations in other sources like Bhagavad Gita, Shiva Samhita etc. Summary of all these reckoning up to my perception, 'A Yogi is someone who seeks the ultimate truth, even though being in the midst of samsara (world, society) but uninfluenced by its conditioning'. Yogi need not be someone who sits in a cave and practice asceticism; it's just one way of many kinds. A meditator, a philosopher, a devotee, a mystic all of them are Yogis. Irrespective of our professions or marital status, all of us can become yogis. Yogi can be in a robe made with silk, or a cassock, or jeans, or even in suits. And Nolan is a yogi in suits. In recent times another yogi who wore suits was J Krishnamurti. There are many reasons for calling Christopher Nolan a Yogi. Below are the expected qualities of a Yogi and it's interesting to know, how this man makes the grade in all of them.

Quest for the reality:

Chris explored and exploring incessantly through both possible ways of science and spirituality. Reaching the depths of mind till the limbo and crossing the galaxies till the black hole Gargantua. Of course there are many psychological thrillers and space sci-fi movies, but if we think how distinct these movies are from others, we surely realize the glory Nolan's way. They are made in such a way that all movie goers should accept with no second opinion. If we take example of Interstellar, there are other epic movies like Gravity and Martian, where in, director portrays the space adventure in a most creative and engaging manner with technical details and wholesome entertainment, those films feed the intellect and heart without any disturbances. In the contrary, in Interstellar we question everything, even the characters probe along with audience which is intriguing. Cooper is a sensible and an authentic man who possesses the same curiosity about space and time as that of the audience, and makes an honest effort to understand their nature. This will rise many questions in the mind of viewers and create a sense of admiration when they get the answers and finally a feeling of enlightenment at the end.

Nolan's movie character's like Leonard Shelby of Memento, Will Dormer of Insomnia, Bruce Wayne the Batman, Dom Cobb of Inception many a times go deep inside retrospectively and question themselves. They create challenges and conflicts on their own and resolve them. This shows Nolan is quite deep in self-analysis which is again a quest for knowing true self or the reality. Characters are the reflections of the creator's mind, his will, desires, regrets, fantasies, and so on.

Solitude of a Karmayogi:

Solitude here need not mean social isolation, in the era where a school kid maintains a twitter handle and where life cannot be imagined without cellphones, Chris Nolan's seclusion from social media is a miracle. At the same time it is an indigestive truth for his fans and followers. He does not own a cellphone and an email account! He thinks, it gives him time to think. In an interview with Hollywood Reporter he says, "Well, I've never used email because I don't find it would help me with anything I'm doing. I just couldn't be bothered about it. As far as the cellphone goes, it's like that whole thing about "in New York City, you're never more than two feet from a rat" - I'm never two feet from a cellphone. I mean, we'll be on a scout with 10 people and all of them have phones, so it's very easy to get in touch with me when people need to. When I started in this business, not many people had cellphones, I didn't have one, I never bothered to get one and I've been very fortunate to be working continuously, so there's always someone around me who can tap me on the shoulder and hand me a phone if they need to. I actually really like not having one because it gives me time to think. You know, when you have a smartphone and you have 10 minutes to spare, you go on it and you start looking at stuff."

He reads printed emails. Very secretive and works stealthily and comes out only after his movie release. He is open to talks and interviews after his product is out. When the whole world fights and debates on his work, he sips his favorite tea in the flask kept in the pocket of his overcoat and smiles.

This dedication in work and apathetic stand towards the fame or social presence is the key essence of a Yogi. Work style of Chris Nolan is exactly the same as, what Shri Krishna advocates about the

Karmayoga in Bhagavad Gita,
karmany evadhikaras te
ma phalesu kadacana
ma karma-phala-hetur bhur
ma te sango stvakarmani   2.47

Yoga-sthah kuru karmani
sangam tyaktva dhananjaya
siddhy-asiddhyoh samo bhutva
samatvam yoga ucyate   2.48

In simple translation it goes like,

Your work is your responsibility,
not its result.
Never let the fruits of your actions
be your motive.
Nor give in to inaction.   2.47

Set firmly in yourself, do your work,
not attached to anything.
Remain even minded in success,
and in failure.
Even mindedness is true yoga.   2.48
—Bhagavad Gita

Ingenuity:

Original ideas can be born only when you are not much influenced by the society. Nolan was inspired by films like, Star Wars and Stanley Kubrick's magnum opus '2001 a Space Odyssey'; early times, and was artistically influenced by graphic artist M.C Eschar and other filmmakers Ridley Scott and David Lean etc. These are all part of learning process and are the roots of creative ignition in him. And when he got all the freedom to direct his own film, he mostly started adapting his own ideas into films, preferred refinement of the existing ideas and to give more dimensions to them. Many a times he succeeded in breaking the conventions by creating characters that are self-deceptive like Leonard Shelby, and nonlinear narrative structure, that demands audience to think. Testimonial for the originality of Chris Nolan is his film Inception, a film that will be discussed and debated for generations. It is a concoction of science, art and philosophy. Interstellar stands no far from it.

A Moralist and Philosopher:

Chris Nolan, right from his first movie, tried to promote morals and in few cases he leaves the decision to the audience, to draw a conclusion of what is right and what is wrong. 'Promoting morality is a quality of moralist and leaving the decision by posing conflict and intrigue is the quality of a philosopher'. We all talk of morality and ethics over a cup of coffee, but we forget, milk used in our coffee was produced for nourishment of a calf by her mother and it was snatched forcefully. All the scriptures and religions give priority for morality, not only because doing so called wrong is bad or cause harm to others in society. But because, when we commit a crime, there will be a deep guilt and regret inside. And that pang of guilt won't help us grow spiritually. It will turn into a hurdle during the course of muzzling the mind which is inevitable to experience the true self.

If we witness the embedded philosophy of Christopher Nolan in his films, we can notice an organic growth of a philosopher in him. Everything starts with suspicion, when we doubt, we become attentive. From the movie Following to Inception, it seems like Nolan belonged to the school of suspicion, just identical to Friedrich Nietzsche or Sigmund Freud. When the man of suspicion becomes optimistic, he will become a Vedantin, that's what we witness in Interstellar.

A great example for Chris Nolan's moralist as well as philosophic approach is Dark Knight Trilogy. 'With an indie filmmaking background, though you have an independent & personal idea to materialize, when you start working for a studio, you have to compromise it', is what is believed by many people. But Chris proved it wrong. He achieved both. The reboot of Batman was a completely new treat for the audience. Instead of keeping a grandeur and fantasy as a core theme; Chris believed in script and made it a best contemporary story which has a strong message. The Dark Knight Trilogy made a true justice to original batman and aggrandized in many aspects that lead to making Batman a more cult and family man. There are many movies with vigilantism, in most cases the stories are driven by revenge or plain savior theme. But Dark Knight series stand entirely unique with all richness.

In the second movie of the trilogy, The Dark Knight, a scene where in Joker propounds that he owns the city; as part of rescue operation, the people in charge load up two ferries with people to get them out of the city. The Joker had wired both boats with explosives and had given each boat the detonator to the other one, saying that he will blow up both boats at midnight if one boat does not blow up the other.

This incident poses the most fundamental question of morality in human beings. Is it ok or good to kill someone, in the fear that you will be killed otherwise? Isn't life equal for all? This scenario is portrayed effectively by trialing it on a crowd in ferry, which audiences feel so familiar with. And also by blending it into a story line, like Joker testing the people of Gotham through his experiment to prove all are selfish and ugly when it comes to death and life, just like himself. But he fails and morality prevails.

In the third installment Dark Knight Rises, there is another scene where, Mr. Bruce Wayne is trapped in an underground prison. There, the inmates tell Wayne the story of Ra's al Ghul's child, who was born and raised in the prison before finally escaping, the only prisoner to have ever done so. Wayne thinks that, if a child could escape, 'why can't I?' Then he gets ready for the climb by doing pushups and body exercises. Ties a big rope around his chest and goes for the climb. He fails when he is just a twelve-foot leap from the rest of the climb and drops a hundred feet - the rope catches, slamming him into the rock face.

In the next attempt, there is a conversation between Wayne and prisoner, where in prisoner says "You do not fear death. You think this makes you strong. This makes you weak!" And then he motivates him to go for climb without the rope. He meant, if you go without rope, in the fear of fall and death, you will surely make it, you should fear the death, so you fight to live. The rope is just a hindrance, it may save you but it will not help you climb.

We have seen many of us saying heroic dialogues like 'I am not afraid of death!' If we really don't have that fear, we may not succeed in this material world. For example: Buddhism is the most practical and beautiful religion for contemporary world because it has neither red stains of violence nor hatred in its history, it may not procure in future too. Buddhist philosophy advocates peace and silence of the mind. It dilutes the emotions of the follower day by day and creates a Buddha in him, a serine and calm being who goes beyond death, death is nothing for him. If you tell him to climb well of that underground prison, he may not be able to, because he doesn't have anything to lose even if he fails to climb. He doesn't have a Gotham city waiting for him to be saved. Nor he is worried of death in there. He might just wake up and sit every day and practice meditation till he leaves the body in the same prison.

Buddhism is the actual Hinduism and seems to be the last hope of survival in this planet. It is a most adaptive, simple, scientific and appealing religion. But it is not for super heroes or the ones who want to achieve something or prove something in this material world around us. So we can embrace it only after we are done with the worldly business. One should have fear of death until he/she achieves something big in this material world. This is how, Chris Nolan's incredible philosophy works.

Grasping heartbeats & Personal yogic features:

It is quite evident that Chris makes films that are both artistically genius and commercially success. His consistency shows that, he well interpreted the heartbeat of the audience. I.e. he has a picture of what the minds of the viewers demand. In order to interpret other's mind and their demands, you need to go deeper. In order to go deeper, you need to understand the depth. That depth can be understood only when you experience it within yourself. You need to go deep inside yourself to seize others. It holds good even in relationships, I need to go deep inside myself to understand my partner deeply.

It is a method of study, 'Just as by the knowledge of one lump of clay we have the knowledge of all the clay in the universe'. If we want to clench the mind of others, we have to know the nature of our own mind. If we have to control other's mind, we have to control our own.

Many people who collaborated and worked with him say that 'he is cold and aloof filled with humility'; when we see Nolan talking, we feel a charm and an aura of a matured gentleman emanating a constant radiation. He speaks with a British accent, giving him an air of sophistication accentuated by his habit of wearing suits, he doesn't speak anything surplus. He chooses favorable words and of course he is from English literature background, but his speeches are like a mystic.

Very few people know that, Chris Nolan is blessed with four children and he must be a great father. Cooper and Murph's intense affection to each other shows it. Emma is a Yogini too, else it wouldn't be possible to produce such great films in grand scale along with supervision of a big family with all composure. Nolan couple is a model and admired by numerous budding filmmaking partners from both east and western part of the world.

Suits every day:

Yogis do not waste time and energy in showing up or making choices on what to wear for the day, so Chris Nolan is no different. Alfred Hitchcock wore suits in set as to show respect for his job and keep up the dignity. But Nolan's case is different; he doesn't want to waste energy in choosing a new attire every day. In one of his DGA interview, his answer for question, 'Why suits every day' was "I went to a boarding school where we had to wear a uniform, and I got used to using all the pockets in my jacket. It's just what I'm comfortable in. I don't like to think about what to wear, so I just wear the same thing every day. When I first started shooting with a crew on Memento I remember trying to pick up a sandbag and everyone was shouting at me that I wasn't allowed to do that because there were specific people for that job. As much as I'd like to be able to get my hands dirty, I don't usually get to do so. So I dress the way I would for a day at the office. It's just easier that way."

It is also evident that Nolan has influenced many people with his decency and he succeeded in bringing everyone to his level of sublimity. His movie sets will have many men with suits and ties as per his close sources.

He is Sthithaprajna:

In chapter 2 we tried to grasp the meaning of sthithaprajna, he is a man with steady wisdom and emotionally controlled. If we see Nolan, he seems to be totally composed and as per the reliable sources around him, he is a captain cool and never shouts in the sets or shows an outburst with anger. Nor goes ecstatic for simple reasons, on top of all this he talks minimal but with lot of weightage.

You create something out of your own world. If we see the works of Nolan, he is there in every character he created. Even the villains in his films are intelligent and have a proper agenda. When someone has to create so composed characters, he should be that first. The consistency in his work and patience to accept the critics after the release of his films prove that, Christopher Nolan is a sage of steady wisdom.

How To Be [come] a Yogi :

Here are the easiest steps to become a yogi in modern world.

- Since the time you are born, there are many conditionings smeared on your mind, it is a sweet conspiracy to manipulate you and turn a product of the so called society or the environment. It starts from the family, as a child you will be totally influenced by the family in terms of caste and religion. They say, you are a Hindu or a Jew. You are a Tatar, descendent or Tartars. You are a Gowda or a Brahmin and so on. Then some programming is done in the chip of your head called morals and ethics, a great belief system is established. They force education on you. All the credits of machinization of man should go to modern education. You are ought to learn certain course and become a doctor or an engineer. Once you get a job, again you have a stereotypical pattern that you need to follow. An agenda for life, you need to marry, especially the girl who belongs to the same caste/religion then a house and children. Right from the childhood you are prepared for a mundane rat race, you will also be induced with certain fears like death, which nobody knows whether it is painful or just a door to the new life, everyone is habituated to cry. So you cry too.

When you are driven by the rules and these conditionings, your life becomes so mechanical, just like the clock. You are compelled by the external forces around and just a walking dead. You do not think much because you do not have scope and time to, there is also a worry that if you stop somewhere and think, you will be lagging behind in the race. When you are placed in a rat race, it is natural that you compare yourself with others, and you will try to better your position. You will start living to prove something to someone. This is where your un-living starts. When your life becomes so automated, you will not have freedom. You just push the time, having governed by the programming made in you. Just drop these conditionings, break the rules silently. Drop doesn't mean, become a freak, drop these ideas from the mind, need not broadcast it to the world, be aware of them. Wherever and whenever possible, try to avoid and get rid of them. Just be a silent samurai, look around and smile. You blossom silently like a wild flower.

How to drop? The moment you are aware of your conditionings, you are wise now. You just know, these are all a temporary adjustments to keep you in rat race. If your religion hinders you anywhere, drop it. Religion should be there to elevate you, not to depress you, just drop in mind. If your profession drags you down, just see a better way to quit it and do what you like to do. If you are too much bound by god and morals, just drop them. If the so called traditions make you duel minded, just drop them. You are impaired from flying due to over burden of these conditionings. Go on dropping, till you feel your wings are light, So that you can soar higher and higher till you reach the glorious sun.

- The moment you drop the conditioning, you will be fearless, you will be a wolf. Once you acquire courage, you will experience an immense freedom. It's your first victory; you will be the most joyful person. Where there is a freedom, happiness follows. Happiness is the goal of freedom.

- When you experience the freedom, you will start living. You govern yourself and start listening to your intuition. The consequence of this will be, you begin to do what you love. No matter how late, no matter how suppressed and buried deep down in you, it comes up. Just accept it. You are never old to do what you like. It is there in a corner of your mind, when you open the door of your intuition, it springs out.

- Now your mind is tranquil and you are following your intuition, you just see yourself. You have achieved something great. You are born again. You are already a Yogi. And you are the happiest person on earth.

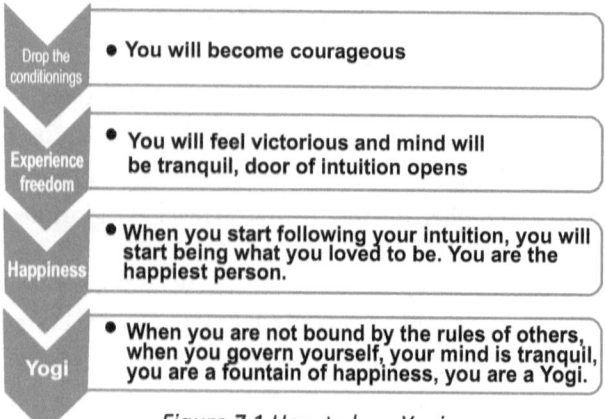

Figure 7.1 How to be a Yogi

There is a song in Japanese film 'Ikiru', which reminds us to find the meaning of life and provokes to follow our intuition! And be a yogi.

life is brief.
fall in love, maidens
before the crimson bloom
fades from your lips
before the tides of passion
cool within you,
for those of you
who know no tomorrow.....

What next after yogi?

One feels, worldly achievements are nothing and then he starts controlling his internal and external nature. When one masters it, he will be at next level of what Patanjali said in RajaYoga, the yogi, who can perform all miracles. One can become anything he wants after becoming a yogi. He can roam all the universe without a spaceship! He lives in his true form, the Christly form.

Fistful of facts about Interstellar

- The character of Murph was originally a boy in early drafts of the script.

- Cooper and Dr. Brand came back to Endurance after 23 years, 4 months and 8 days. Which means that their entire mission on Miller's planet took some 3 hours 17 minutes.

- After the crew landed on Miller's planet, just when they are about to get off Ranger 1, the score softens, and we can hear ticks approximately once every second. Because of the time dilation due to Gargantua's gravity, every tick represents approx. 17 hours on earth.

- Actor Matt Damon was not included in the promotion for the film. His name was not mentioned and he did not attend any of the premieres. In fact, apart from an article in Variety announcing his casting as an "unspecified role," his role was kept secret until the release of the film.

- In the film, the characters are from five different continents across the globe, performing a major heist. Cobb, Arthur, and Mal are from the U.S. (N. America). Cobb fetches Ariadne from Paris, France (Europe); Eames and Yusuf are from Mombasa (Africa). Saito is from Japan (Asia), and Fischer is from Australia.

Chapter

Art: The universal religion

"The last hope for the comprehensive evolution of humanity is Art
                                                                -Author

Man is evolved with the aid of his own thoughts and accumulated knowledge of the society. Philosophers said, man is a rational and social animal. There was an inevitability of a common code of conduct and some ethical principles for the better living among the communities, and hence the religions were born. They were nurtured with the help of baffling mystery called 'death' and with moral traits like sins, good, bad, sacred, unholy, guilt and so on. Clergymen succeeded in indulging some amount of fear and respect about god by using these morals and ethics as their weapons. Eventually many religions were established geographically throughout the world, they act as protocols for the living among respective societies, but all of them do not provide a sort of ultimacy or transcendence. When the man started invading other's colonies, there were collisions of culture and faiths. Especially in countries like India and America, many immigrants came and settled belonging to foreign religions. Therefore communal harmony is an expected quality of a democratic country. As the democracy evolved, everybody has got their own freedom of expression and practice. Conflicts are expected in such conditions, but if such misunderstanding leads to a disorder in the society, it may become a serious global crisis in long run.

Religions are started to create coherence among the people but today they are becoming the reason for riots! Instead of elevating the minds with their noble ideas and philosophy, they are degrading the minds. As we observed in 21st century, we witnessed a proliferation of Islamic groups that preach fanaticism, violent extremism and became a global issue; it's also evident that there is sexual extremism in the catholic church and issue of intolerance in other religions. These facts have helped place religion in a very unfavorable light. There is no surprise if it leads to rise of anti-religion sentiments throughout the world in future.

Why the religions are failed?

There can be many reasons for a failure; if we look at any of these reasons individually they may not seem as the sole contenders but as a group, yes they are. First and foremost thing we should understand here is, religion is purely a personal affair. It is left to the intellectual freedom of individuals. It's just like, I like Robert Di Nero and Leo Dicaprio as actors; or I like ice cream with butterscotch flavor. There is no point debating it in public. It's my choice. I am very much comfortable and compatible with it. If my Dad or Mom liked strawberry flavor, it doesn't mean I should eat the same. It's their life their taste so the mine.

In today's world, any kind of expression of thought in any form is evaluated before being perceived. There is a lot of skepticism, not about the thought but about the person who puts it forward. If someone stands up and says something, we tend to find out, who is he? Why he says that? What is his motif? What religion does he belong to? What is his political agenda hidden behind? Etc. The world suffers from the intolerance. Its regretful to know that being in an era of most advanced civilization, we are still so much conditioned and behave like the frogs of well. If a Hindu says something substantial even in a scientific way, an Islamic doesn't want to hear and think of it. If a Christian priest wants to go for a peace lecture tour, he will be banned by the people of other religion saying, he is a proselytizing agent and coming for the conversion and so on.

We need to see an example for a better apprehension. Yoga (Yogasana in this context) is an ancient physical and mental exercise for a healthy and happy life. It is one of the gifts from India to the world, recently it is promoted well in a global level by the leaders and the UN(United Nations) was convinced to celebrate international Yoga day on 21st of June every year. As everybody knows, Yoga is a discipline of day to day life. It involves certain postures and breathing exercises to keep ourselves fit. It is a great way of keeping mind and body in a healthy and harmonized state. Now, has it got anything to do with any religion? Few fanatics think that it belongs to Hinduism alone!, it was recently in news that, a Muslim girl was assaulted for teaching Yoga to her friends !. What to call for such absurdity. If the religion is too blind to see the truth, why do we need one Are we ready to sacrifice electricity and bulb? Because they are invented by Christians!. They are ok and fine to go for gymnasium but not Yoga. This conservative mindset will not yield any fruits for the future but will create more gaps between the culture and people.

In order to understand, why the religions have lost their sheen and have become foundations for a wall of hatred between the minds, let's take example of India, a land of cultural mishmash. Unity in diversity is the true genius of India and it's an intrinsic nature of Indian soil. Throughout the history, we never see an Indian king invading other countries for the sake of wealth or power, however we see there are hundreds of foreign kings invaded India and have looted her in all aspects. India offered what she had, and given shelter for every alien empire that flourished in her laps with utmost majestic hospitality and motherly pamper. The result being, numerous religions and castes present in India of today. It doesn't mean, conflicts arose only after Islamic invasion, they were there before as well, for example, like Vaishnavas and Shaivas, and before that the system of four Varnas in Vedic society with respect to castes etc.

Politicization:

When we have a vibrant nation possessing multiple religions

with majority, conflicts are common and certain, conflicts in the mind, but not external. Religion is a personal and private choice of man, and that is what we call freedom in simple words. If my brother goes to the mosque and my sister goes to church and I go to temple, is there any problem? We are in the same family; it doesn't mean we should avoid eating together and having fun. The difference in religious views should not create cracks in our relationship. It's just like, my favorite author is Leo Tolstoy and my brother's being Khalil Gibran. I need not force him to read Tolstoy or I need not quarrel with him saying Tolstoy is the only genius. If he likes to read, he will explore. Fortunately no such quarrel is happening as far as authors are concerned. Then why is it a problem with religions?

Because religion is no more a personal business, it's a brand and a cause to win elections. In Indian constitution religion is separate from the state but not from politics. It's completely politicized. Rama and Krishna are used as star campaigners in elections. Few political parties want to convert the religious beliefs into votes; religions have become a means to connect to people. They say 'We will build the temple of your god, so vote for us', another party will say, 'we will build mosques and protect churches, we shall also protect the rights of reservation of minorities and provide more privileges' etc., and hence the religion is utterly politicized. If certain religious groups with the help of a political party pursue power to "impose laws," to force their own ideology as knowledge and discriminate against those who are unlike them, then it will be malicious.

Another way of politicizing the religion is, through donations and bogus charities to the religious organizations. During their tenure in government, few parties release lot of funds to some selected religious establishments having high reputation, so that religious heads from these groups will remain loyal to the ruling party and campaign for them in elections.

When the party forms a government, they will only think in terms of their pre-election promises and the vested interests of few sycophants. Those who are lost will start feeling panic for a while but later will find means to tackle and fight the ruling government then the false allegations will start, and the planned communal riots to show that the government is intolerant and barbaric. The supporters of ruling party will be the kings of the world, and will loosen their tongue and begin to abuse or inferiorize other religions then the game begins. In his uncompleted book, Shri Swami Vivekananda says, *"In other lands this has been attempted by "force", that is, the enforcement of the culture of one race only over the rest, the result being the production of a short-lived vigorous national life; then, dissolution."* When the religion came out from the heart into the streets, the fate of the people is changed. If the same trend continues, the so called God will be identified with the political party in near future.

Commercialization:

God is not free in 21st century, more expensive than any time before in the past. God is commercialized in all possible ways. You have to book flights in season, and there are separate tickets available for Darshan(sight of god in the sanctum), and different rates for different Sevas in the Menu board,(The board looks like a food menu in a five star hotel). After reaching god's abode, it's a pure business again. A trade of offering and the boon. For example a businessman donates an ornament to decorate the god, which is worth of 1 million rupees, he expects god to sanction him a big project/contract worth of 100 million at least. And he will come to fame overnight as a supreme devotee of that god and a prime patron of the temple trust, the trust or the maintainers of that temple will give him special privileges to see the god whenever he wishes to and so on. Even in the Abrahamic religions you have to visit certain places and then only your life will be complete. They say they are against the idolatry but go far away to see an idol itself. This is used as an opportunity for business, so things work in the way of money. Buddha was purely against the idolatry and it is an irony that we see the idols of Buddha most of the places. Idolatry can be accepted, because it creates a means to reach god, as the god is inconceivable to the sense organs, man found a way to objectify him and then through that means, it is easy to conceive the inconceivable.

However commercialization makes god mere an object of trade, like you can buy god if you have money. The rich people can go and visit more places in auspicious occasions, so only those will be blessed by god(!?). We all have to come out of this superstitious and commercial god. If you call yourself children of god, then you have godliness in you too, let's try to realize that godliness within, before going to places to see and appreciate the manmade gods. A 12th century social reformer and a great philosopher Basvanna says,

"The rich will make temples for Shiva,
What shall I, a poor man do? My legs are pillars,
the body the shrine, the head a cupola of gold."

God is within this very body and the body is the temple. Holy ideals are the prayers to him and the work of art is procession of god within.

Heroes of chaos: Fanaticism

All the religions are prospered by propagation of their thoughts and spreading their light to many regions and the people. It is the duty of religious leaders to create harmony and embrace everyone, but majority of the contemporary leaders are too hollow to understand the true sense and intention of religions, they have become a 2Gigabyte memory cards with mugged up information about their respective religions. They have the proselytizing attitude and narrow mindedness which will lead to an increased fanaticism. When people become fanatics, there is no hope for spiritual growth or a social harmony. It will create more gaps among the people and will alienate from fellow human beings belonging to different religions.

It is evident that, there were bomb blasts in Bangladesh in the year 2016 and the attacker was influenced and provoked by preaching of a fanatic religious leader, many internal disturbances, riots, communal violence in the name of religion are everyday news in India. Cow is no more an animal but a symbol for fight and intolerance. Where are we heading to?

It is the job of religious leaders to provide insights about truth and appreciate all the religions, as all of them are proved to be leading to the same light of truth, instead of working for some ordinary vested interests. As a matter of fact, many of such representatives do not praise other religions in the fear that, they might lose the faith of their own followers. Therefore rather than saying I am great or my well is big, we should learn to accept a universal religion. The religious leaders should bring best out of man but not worst out of religion.

Abrahamic religions are interested in conversion with paid missionaries and mafia. Others are interested in establishing their own empire ignoring the minorities. In a country like India, there is no other way but to live in harmony and tolerance than fighting for the so called proof/infallibility of one over other religions. All of our religious leaders should say 'We are all one' as a substitute to their provocative speeches. We should approach the truth/god practically instead of believing an imaginary hell or heaven. India had seen the masters like Shri Ramakrishna, who proposed and professed universal religion by uniting all. Most of the modern leaders have their alliances with the political parties or an organization hence they look for some aids for their actions, and it will defeat the very purpose of the religion.

As the sages quoted in Upanishads, ' "Ekam sat viprabahuda vadanti" "That which exists is one, sages call it by various names." ' All religions lead to the same light and have their own path and nature, person from one religion need not follow other's but, should not cultivate animosity at the same time. All the religions impart acceptance and intolerance towards other religions, prime goal of each of them is to understand the nature of existence and realize the god within.

Media a bad medium:

Media is considered as the fourth pillar of a democracy, freedom to expression is one of the fundamental rights of the citizen in all the republics. After the advent of internet, it went in a new direction all together. Everyone got a chance to express their opinion through social media. And it is also being used to create campaigns, groups, topics etc. For example there are pages in Facebook that have millions of followers, and it is easy to communicate to many people whether it's a good message or a bad one, but the fortune lies in the creator's hand. If the creator is of good motives, well read and socially responsible he/she might promulgate good thoughts. If not, the seeds of bad ideas, communal hatred can be sown easily. Since the religions are politicized, It is obvious that there will be campaigns of hatred. Mostly, social media has become a platform for the same.

Collective identity :

There is a serious concern that should be debated. When a boy opens a facebook/twiiter account, he sees is the heroism and grandeur of such groups/communities. He will be attracted and starts following it. It cripples his intellectual growth. He might not think beyond his communal group. He will continue to spread its ideologies through his smartphone, he even doesn't know what is it saying or what are its implications. He will spend his labor in communication but not thinking independently. It's better to send teenagers on a date than to absurd communal groups. We are the civilization with all cutting-edge technologies, but we still could not separate politics and religion. We fly high till the blackholes but still could not get rid of superstitions and social evils like racism, casteism and regionalism. These all stand to be persistent myths of a ism of modernism.

All of these factors may lead to an aversion towards religion to the future generations! The so called crisis of faith is expected, what is the solution?

An unfulfilled dream:

There was a monk who had a dream, who himself is dream of many. He is the reality of dream and dream of reality. He rose from finite to infinite. He is the sun(son) of India and the Moon for the world. His dream was a dream of nation and a dream for the world full of reality. He was neither a man nor a god but a movement. A crusade that lives forever! He preached divinity within man and revealed how to realize it.

Shri Swami Vivekananda(1863-1902) was one of the greatest monks from India who revamped Hinduism and voiced it throughout the world. Indian history cannot be imagined without Swamiji. Nobel laureate, the mystic poet Rabindranath Tagore rightly said, *"If you want to know India, study swami Vivekananda"*. In 1900 swamiji had predicted that India will be free in next 50 years. Yes he was right, she is free. Every day hundreds of souls in India today are getting inspired by his thoughts. Many wake up in the morning looking at his quote on wall poster, *"Arise, Awake stop not till the goal is reached"*.

We, As normal human beings cannot escape time, hence we are bound to change, many things changed in these 100+ years post his departure. The Russian revolution, Theory of relativity ,The world wars that splashed the world map with the blood, India's independence, Sputnik, Apollo11,Computers,Y2K,Apple,Mobile phones, Donald Trump and so on. Along with the world, India has been transformed in all possible facets like never anticipated before. Indians are ruling the world in the field of technology and business (as the product of western imitation?). Nevertheless there is an unfulfilled dream.

Swamiji had dreamt that, the glory of India being the master for the entire world, the torch bearer for the uncertain future of this planet. He wished everyone should be enlightened by embracing the Vedantic life *'The principles of the Vedanta not only should be preached everywhere in India, but also outside. Our thought must enter into the make-up of the minds of every nation, not through writings, but through persons.'* RamaKrishna Mission alone is fighting for this cause. We as a nation failed to fulfill his dream and it seems like we have taken the opposite direction.

If we observe Swamiji's life and teachings, for Indians he emphasized more on teaching the service to mankind, to uplift poor, and help them get bread, whereas in his western tours, he advocated the core of Vedanta and Upanishads. Why?

India was suffering from hunger, what Indian needed then was the bread to survive, while westerners were swaggering with their achievement in terms of luxury as a product of industrial revolution. The materialism was at its zenith point. Their hunger for food was fulfilled and they wanted something beyond materialistic and sensual pleasures. Vivekananda illuminated them with the genuine and ultimate wisdom of Vedanta in a very appealing way.

How about today? After 100+ years of his leaving, there is still poverty, few are materially poor and others are mentally poor. If we keep aside the unrealistic and politically motivated surveys, the satisfactory thing is, everyone gets adequate food. Almost all have electricity, mobile phones and majority of them have got access to the internet. The trend is, people with lower income are trying to compete with middle class and the middle class are hoping for class of upper strata, their glamour and fantasies. There will never be a time where there is total economic equilibrium. This gap between Roti and Pizza, or the financial imbalance is due to loopholes in the administrative system and also the greed. It will continue for no reason. The problem is, there is a misconception that the growth in life is just the improvement of material luxury. The intellectual and spiritual progress is utterly neglected.

If Swami Vivekananda comes alive ....

Swamiji is already immortal with his missilic thoughts, why should we invoke him again ? what is the necessity ? Is there a need? Yes. There is urgency. The Hinduism what Shankara and Swami

Vivekananda preached is completely warped now. The global impression about Hinduism throughout world is changing since when it's misemployed for politics. Swamiji should come alive to tell the 'Amruthaputras' that, shouting the slogan and running with a saffron colored flag is not Hinduism, Its more deep and more subtle. He observes in his unfinished book notes that *'Monotheism like absolute monarchy is quick in executing orders, and a great centralization of force, but it grows no farther, and its worst feature is its cruelty and persecution. All nations coming within its influence perish very soon after a flaring up of a few years.'* Therefore we should keep our steps wisely.

It is unfortunate for Hindu's that the pulps of Hinduism, Upanishads and commentaries on them are obscured like an eclipsed sun. There is a campaign to portray a saffron mercury bulb as the Sun! Hinduism of today is depicted as a political outfit and a device of propaganda, this process creates a different impression about this holy religion to other sects and religions of the world. It is OK to some extent if it is used only for the elections, but that's not the case here, even after the government is formed, the same campaign is getting continued instead of fundamental issues of a democracy. For example: recently cow had become a great topic of debate and discussion in India. The governments and people alike discussed on cow, instead of sensible issues like farmer suicides, rampant unemployment, unequal education, health concerns, rural infrastructure etc. We should protect cows, instead of looking from the mythological perspective, even if we see logically, Its one of the sublime creatures, from the times of Vedas, cow was the companion of human being which helped him in all ways. We should protect them as we can survive with grains, vegetables, fruits and cereals. It's also not good to kill animal with a divinely consciousness. Its interesting to see Swamiji's view related to this issue, once, a member of a cow protection organization met Swami Vivekananda. He presented him with a picture of cow and explained to him how his organization has been rescuing old cows that are being sent for slaughter.

Swami Vivekananda read the Pamphlet, and asked "Is your organization doing anything to help those dying in the Middle India from the famine? There are already more than 1,00,000 dead." "No, Sir." he replied, "Our organization only take cares of Cows." "Don't you think you should be helping humans? Surely you can save a lot with the funds you collect." Reasoned Swamiji. "No Sir, they are responsible for their condition." said the man. "By that logic, even Cows are being butchered because of their own fate, they don't need our help." said Swamiji with anger. All of the lives are precious, human life should be the first priority. That's the reason we do not eat human meat!, We should protect animals as well, but human being is the only form in the hierarchy that can realize the truth. Here we should also observe that there was a cow in the Ashrama of mystic, his holiness Shri Ramana Maharshi. She got enlightened by the virtue of being in Maharshi's company. We should protect cows! Not because they are superior to us, but because we are superior to them.

Few scholars might debate that it is featured in directive principles of state policy of Indian constitution, that cow should be protected, it is true. The same way, it is also mentioned that 'State shall endeavor to bring about prohibition of the consumption except for medicinal purposes of intoxicating drinks and of drugs which are injurious to health'. So why don't you debate over liquor ban throughout the nation, which is causing more serious mental and physical illness for the people.

The policies of the government should uphold the human rights and help its citizens prosper in all the aspects that lead to an inclusive and comprehensive growth. All citizens should also be wise to understand whenever the political parties play with their religious faiths and feelings instead of the core issues of the people. Vedanta has solution for all the problems of human life, but it cannot provoke people like other religions it preaches the principle but not a person. Hence no materialistic gains can be made with it. Therefore it cannot become a universal religion. It is a sharp sword under the saffron scabbard.

The last hope could have been Buddhism, the most practical contemporary religion. There is no surprise that many management Gurus and Film stars are silently embracing Buddhism. It's clean and crisp. There is no time anywhere in the past that people fought due to this religion, nor there any examples of forceful conversions; nowhere stained with blood; but it's too simple to believe! People need something complicated with lot of contradictions. In India this also was made like every other religion as used by certain classes of people. Dr. Ambedkar had a noble thought when he revamped it. The upper strata of the society doesn't like Buddhism as its too dull, nothing aggressive in there, cannot create any issues with silence, there is no opportunity to create chaos and organize people and build a party.

So the ultimate solution is....

When religions fail, art and science should take up the responsibility of spiritual evolution of human mind. Art is the only medium that can make people think, provide the insights and convey truth. A vedantist monk, wearing saffron robe might stand to give a lecture about some sublime concept of prana and akasha , the truth of existence, a Muslim/Christian will hesitate to attend the lecture because the speaker is a Hindu. It's a saffron robe that he wears. However everyone will rush to watch Christopher Nolan's movie, even he talks about same concept. No one will have any problem, Why? Here wins the art!.

Shri. Albert Einstein in his autobiographical account, 'The world as I see It', notes it one hundred years ago, he says *"How can cosmic religious feeling be communicated from one person to another, It can give no definite notion of a God and no theology? In my view it is the most important function of art and science to awaken this feeling and keep it alive in those who are capable of it*". How true! We need art and science in modern world for this very reason.

If the humanity has to progress, Art must be given emphasis than any other fields. Commerce helps you survive materially; Philosophy feeds your intellect, it argues and instructs, it helps you grow intellectually; religion may exhort and command you; but art alone is the abode of bliss, its language is happiness, it delights you every time, when you go in contact with it. The aesthetic emotion is the true spiritual experience, not a mere subjective feeling. Sufism is one of the greatest ways to attain the truth, It is a synthesis of art and Bhaktivedanta. One of the finest songs to come out from the inspiration of Sufism in popular culture is 'Kun Fayakun' from Rockstar, It is composed with the true Sufi spirit by the mystic composer AR Rehman and it is dedicated to the great Sufi saint Nizamuddin Auliya. The term Kun Fayakun means ' Be, it is'. It appeared in holy Quran in reference to Allah's Glorious creation powers.

"*The originator of the heavens and the earth, when he decrees a matter, he only says to it: Be! and it is.*"

In the subjective perspective of a man it can also be interpreted as 'You be and it is' If you want something just be that. If you desire to attain the truth, be the truth. Both connotations hold good, our motive is to appreciate and experience the Allah through the art, but not to debate upon it to downgrade ourselves. Below are the first two verses of the song.

>Jab Kahin Pe Kuch Nahi.
>Bhi Nahi Tha
>Wahi Tha Wahi Tha
>Wahi Tha Wahi Tha

>When, there was nothing,
>He was the one,
>the only one.

> Woh Jo Mujh Mein Samaya
> Woh Jo Tujh Mein Samaya
> Maula Wahi Wahi Maaya
>
> He is the one who is manifested in me,
> He is the one, manifested in you,
> O dear Lord, He is the one that is mystery

The song expresses the intuition of the singer who adores the unmanifested truth. The singer sees the unity of manifested and the unmanifested, and venerates the creator for it. He sings to embrace and become one with the god.

Apart from its aesthetic emotion, the song springs an Upanishadic direct experience of god in the soul of listener. It says, he was there before the time and creation or before the big bang! And he is the one who is manifested in everyone and expressed through everything. He is the absolute, that one ultimate reality, the Lord, the Allah, the Brahman.

When a thought is expressed in the form of art, it goes right into the heart. Art is a freeway to reach the soul. It opens all the doors of our being that are shunned from the ages with the name of religions or the morals, the doctrines or the dogmas. It gives solace and it is the solace in itself. The appeal of the artist coerces into acquiescence those who cannot grasp the reasoning of philosophy or do not agree with infallibility of scriptures. If the truth of the existence cannot be infused into a man's head by the engines of argument and proof, the beauty of the creation of an artist may yet win a way to the heart, and succeed. Man sinks into silence in the aura and fragrance of the music.

Who is a true artist?

Artist is an artist, he is the truth, and how can there be a true artist? We should pursue the worldly method to discover the artist, the true artist; He is not someone who swims in the Indian Ocean or the Pacific Ocean, he doesn't compartmentalize, he is a free shark who swims through all waters of the world as one sea. He is not someone who identifies himself with a race or caste or creed, We often hear the words 'A black filmmaker' or a 'Dalit poet', If the artist confines himself inside these dark walls, how can he claim himself/herself to be a true artist? All the creation from such man will be prejudiced and colored with his own limited notions. The true artist is like an eagle, which soars higher and higher and observes without any discriminations or earthly influences, he is the 'saakshi prajna' a witness. He responds with the intuition and creates with universal appeal. All the people need not become true artists, lets first become a man and an artist and then the true artist in the final phase. The true artist is the truth in him.

Many true artists have walked on this planet, who had a third eye of art, who could express their insights, and could write with the highest philosophical and spiritual content, be it Tagore or Kuvempu, Gibran or Tolstoy, the art had true meaning; Paintings of Ravi Varma, Picasso, Da Vinci and Vincent Van Gogh and so on, speak to themselves, they are the expressions from the soul; The compositions of Beethoven, Ravishankar, Ennio Morricone still reverberate and echo through many depths; 'Cinema Paradiso', 'Bicycle Thief' convey what is art in the Cinema. These men have proved that the art alone can touch the souls, if you just notice, anything that you call religious is an art in its sublime form. The great Upanishads are pure poetry that has the ability touch the soul directly.

Christopher Nolan is one of such true artists. Mind of the audience is his canvas, and he splashes the colors from the palette of his subconscious, then he connects the dots with the brush of his intuition, there you see, a living painting. Chris Nolan fills up his entire experience, thoughts and intuition into the work he does. His subconscious is a rich heritage of science, philosophy and poetry. He is a masterpiece of the creator. As a true artist he is undertaking the work of all the religions, all the Churches, Temples and Mosques and priests, popes, moulas, acharyas, swamijis of the world. If we accept art as a universal religion, then Christopher Nolan is the messenger of 21st century.

Fistful of facts about Interstellar

- All robots names in Interstellar are anagram. TARS, KIPP & CASE. TARS is anagram for STAR. KIPP is anagram for KIP (Kip Thorne). CASE (if you add 'P' from KIPP to it) is anagram for SPACE.

- The apocalyptic Earth setting in this film is inspired by the Dust Bowl disaster that took place in the United States during the Great Depression in the 1930s.

- The majority of shots of the robot TARS were not computer generated. Rather TARS was a practical puppet controlled and voiced on set by Bill Irwin who was then digitally erased from the film. Irwin also puppeteered the robot CASE, but in that instance had his voice dubbed over by Josh Stewart.

- For a cornfield scene, Christopher Nolan sought to grow 500 acres of corn, which he learned was feasible from his producing of Man of Steel (2013). The corn was then sold and he actually made a profit.

Chapter 9

Chase Your Reality

"Enough chasing dreams, No more sedatives! It's time to awake, we need stimulatives"   -Author

When the whole world still says "Chase your dreams", Christopher Nolan in one of his latest speeches in Princeton University, said *"Chase your reality".* Though he said it referring to the climax scene of the movie Inception, it is one of the most astounding statements made (Just like 'tat tvam asi' of modern era). There are no less than a million books on how to chase your dreams, but none on how to chase the reality. We take it for granted that we are in reality and start talking about dreams, but how can the changing world be real? All the sky scrapers and architectural wonders will fall down some day, just the way it happened in Cob and Mal's shared dream. And the way the flower withers away by evening, this very body that we are hosted will perish too. Even the gigantic stars turn into black holes; still we think and live like we are going to live forever in this material world with this impermanent body.

It's time to think and understand 'What is the goal of this life?' What is the reason for all this craving? What is this corporate marathon for? Why is this eagerness for self-identity? Why is this continuous hankering and excitement for social success? What is this sordid, materialist, and utilitarian life for? One answer for all questions is Happiness. Yes, man is seeking happiness! What is happiness? It's an eternal breeze with a divine Jasminic odor emanating from the soul. Happiness is a state of mind! It's an everlasting joy and infinite bliss. How can the words describe happiness? It has to be felt and experienced. Majority of us have misconceived happiness. We chase pleasure and gratification instead of happiness. Pleasure is momentary, a temporary phenomenon whereas the happiness is eternal, a simple logic to cognize here is, "You attain finite from the finite, achieve infinite from infinite alone". If we are driven by the materialistic desires, how can we obtain perpetual bliss? The very nature of the matter is temporary. The material adjunct in us can be satisfied with matter, the body and mind are contented with the money, relationships and fame. These things cause momentary sensual gratification but not the ultimate bliss. There is an essence of eternal spirit in every one of us, and how can it be satisfied with transitory pleasures? Now the question is how to attain this eternal joy? Nowhere to go! And there is nothing to attain, it's already there immanent in the self, just needs to be revealed. It is one of the intrinsic attributes of the self. As we already know, nature of the self is Sachidananda (Sat the Existence + Chit the Consciousness + Ananda the Bliss). The bliss manifests once in a while for some of us, because it's veiled by the illusion of external material world or Maya which is created through mind. When the objective world disappears, the sun rises in the midnight. The reality is revealed like the charming and silvery rays of a full moon sink in you from the aperture of a small and lonely hut on top of a hill, everything is illumined in an eternal silence.

Is it easy to get rid of the objective world? It's not as simple as closing the eyes. It needs little more effort, one more subsequent step, opening of the inner eyes. Objective world doesn't exist without the subjective mind. 'The World doesn't exist when 'I' die'. Mind exists only when we think, so what we think is what matters. We think based on our conditionings and Samskara's or the psychological imprints. Our beliefs, faiths, desires, stereotypes, dogmas, superstitions, forced morals bind us to the objective world. Once all of them are dropped, one by one like yellow leaves from a tree, there will be a birth of new foliage and fresh bloom. Wings of the caged bird will be rejuvenated, and the freedom is at the doorstep, sky is not the limit to soar. Sacred ideals and principles are to be used as the propellants to the rocket; they should also be dropped later, like the stage separation one after the other, and rocket alone has to cross the galaxies at the speed of light and become one with this enigmatic universe. It's easy to drop the conditionings, but only when we know them. A completely understood problem is half answered.

It's of no use if a man lives like a machine. Man made machines, and machines made man a machine! He is driven by a routine and programmed with a corporate code; deficient of intellectual material and his soul is shrinking from the famine of spirit. He forgot his wings and living like a primitive creature. He is more interested on the dust of land than the twinkling stars in the sky. His fierce eagerness for the wealth and fame has made him a mad monkey. When his whole attention is on the valley of materialism, how can he climb the radiant hill of spirituality and kiss the sky of immortal heaven? We have countless examples in the history, the fate of those mortal men, who chased matter. Life of Alexander the Great is a testimony. Though we know the story, it's worth recollecting as a reminder. Alexander was a great Greek king. As a military commander, he was undefeated and the most successful monarch throughout history. On his way home from conquering many kingdoms, he came down with an illness. The very moment, all of his captured territories, powerful army, golden throne, sharp swords and the wealth looked futile to him. He realized that death would soon arrive and he would be unable to return to his homeland. He told his generals: "I will soon leave this world. I have three final wishes. You need to carry out what I tell you." His officers, in tears, agreed.

"My first wish is to have my physician bring my coffin home alone". After a gasping for air, Alexander continued: "My second wish is scatter the gold, silver, and gems from my treasure-house along the path to the tomb when you ship my coffin to the grave." After wrapping in a woolen blanket and resting for a while, he said: "My final wish it to put my hands outside the coffin." People surrounding him all were very curious, but no one dared to ask the reason. Alexander's most favored general kissed his hand and asked: "My Majesty, We will follow your instruction. But can you tell us why you want us to do it this way?" After taking a deep breath, Alexander said: "I want everyone to understand the three lessons I have learned. To let my physician carry my coffin alone is to let people realize that a physician cannot really cure people's illness. Especially when they face death, the physicians are powerless. I hope people will learn to treasure their lives. My second wish is to tell people not to be like me in pursuing wealth. I spent my whole life pursuing wealth, but I was wasting my time all through. My third wish to let people understand that I came to this world in empty hands and I will leave this world also in empty hands." he closed his eyes after finished talking and stopped breathing.

We are all Alexanders in a way, we are busy 24 hours for no reason, and we take grave decisions for the sake of accumulating wealth. We are yearning for fame at the cost of our lives. One Alexander is fair enough for this world. Foolish become an example of fallacy and wisemen learn from them. But what we see all throughout the road are victims. There are people who live and die of lust for women, there are people who live and die for the material wealth, but there is no one who lives and dies for the god/truth.

We cannot ignore or evade fortune; no one has to be a monk here. We need material success as well, but not in the cost of happiness. Material aspiration should not induce a restless marathon and a groping in the dark. One must lead a blissful and modest life. Recently, there was an interesting news about the great scientist cum philosopher Albert Einstein. Well, he is more in news these days, but this time not for his gravitational waves or any other scientific invention. It's for his "Theory of Happiness". In 1922, Einstein was at the Imperial Hotel in Tokyo Japan, where he was on a lecture tour, and had recently learned that he had won the Nobel Prize. When a bellboy delivered a message to the physicist, he fished in his pocket for some change to tip him and came up empty. Instead, Einstein offered a tip in the form of his theory on how to live a happy life *"A calm and modest life brings more happiness than the pursuit of success combined with constant restlessness,"* he wrote in German on a piece of hotel stationery.

Authors of most of the personality development books have lead a life full of struggle and restlessness, they wrote their methods and laws, and it became a tradition later. This doesn't mean that, the readers have to go through the same tussle. Our view of success has to be changed. What is success? It's not mere wealth or fame or the combination of both. If that would have been the case, son/daughter of a banker or a celebrity would have been happier than anyone else in the world. The happiness is within and the moment we feel it, we are a success. Even a porn star becomes popular in the social media with more followers than the president or a poet! Is it really needed? Do we have to become popular at the cost of life? Is that all real? These are the questions we need to ask ourselves. Is it not foolishness to equate success to wealth and fame? In fact these two will take man far away from the success. Wealth brings selfishness in man and the fame builds up ego. When someone has both, how can he lead a happy life?

Now it is pertinent to see, how the problem of man can be solved by the fusion of Nolan's works and Vedanta philosophy. Just to recap, the fundamental problem that man facing today is being unhappy despite all the comforts, due to the alienation or the estrangement from the self. The solution is, assessment of present situation in life, cultivating the attitude of questioning. Once we question what is happening, where am I, what am I doing, why am I doing, where am I heading to etc. arise in the mind, it is the first step towards the truth. The question is the seed of intellectual evolution, when we become aware of goings-on in life, we become wise, from wise comes the wisdom, and wisdom leads to the truth. As soon as the fundamental questions are answered, one ultimate problem hovers over the head, that is, what is the reality? What is my nature? Where will I go once I die?

It is appreciable that Vedanta is much practical and can even be practiced by a layman leading a humdrum life; on the contrary, all the western philosophies are just the armchair efforts to find the truth in the purview of intellect by hypothesis and reasoning. There is a very well-known story in India; it is reiterated in many spiritual congregations wherever the speaker talks about the 'reality' of our existence.

Once upon a time in India, there lived a great king Janaka who ruled over the country of Videha. It was the middle of the day when he had a short nap for a few minutes, he dreamt that a rival king with a huge army had invaded his country and massacred his soldiers and ministers. He was driven out of his palace barefooted and without any clothes left over him.

Janaka found himself in a forest roaming with thirst and hunger. He reached a small town where he begged for food. No one paid any attention to his pleas. He reached a place where some people were distributing food to the beggars. Each beggar had an earthen bowl to receive rice water. Janaka had no bowl and so they turned him out to bring a bowl. He went in search of a vessel, requested other beggars to lend him a bowl. But none would part with their bowls. At last Janaka found a broken piece of a bowl. Then he ran to the spot where rice water was distributed. All the food stuff had been already distributed.

King Janaka was drained of long travelling and scorching heat of summer. He stretched himself near a fireplace where foodstuff was cooked. Here someone took pity over Janaka. She gave him some rice water which was found at the bottom of a vessel. Janaka took it with intense joy. When the rice water was about to touch his lips, two large bulls tumbled fighting over him. The bowl was broken to pieces. The king woke up with great fear.

Janaka was trembling violently. He was in a great dilemma as to which of his two states was real. All the time he was in dream, he never thought that it was an illusion and that the misery of hunger and thirst and his other troubles were unreal.

The queen asked Janaka, "O Lord! What is the matter with you?" The only words that Janaka spoke were, "Which is real, this or that?" From that time he left all his work and became traumatized. He uttered nothing but the above words.

The ministers thought that Janaka was suffering from some disease. It was announced by them that anyone who cured the king will be rewarded and those who fail to cure the king will be made life prisoners. Great physicians and specialists began to pour in and tried their luck, but no one could answer the query of the king. Hundreds of Brahmins well versed in medicine and psychology were put in the state prison.

Among the prisoners was also the father of the great sage Ashtavakra. Legends say that Ashtavakra was born with eight physical handicaps due to his father's curse. His name literally means 'eight bends'. According to one version of the folklores, his father was once reciting the Vedas, but erred in correct intonation, Ashtavakra heard it from his mother's womb, the fetus corrected his father; the father got angry and cursed him. The curse caused him to be born crooked.

When Ashtavakra was a boy of only ten years, he was told by his mother that his father was a state prisoner because he failed to cure king Janaka. He at once started to see Janaka. There was a great laughter on Ashtavakra when he entered the court of Janaka. All court men tried to ridicule Ashtavakra over his physical impairments. Ashtavakra did not feel humiliated but laughed back over the assembly with a pity. Janaka asked the reason for his laughter, and Ashtavakra replied, "Don't your pundits know that body is just a vehicle and 'I' am Brahman? I feel pity on this kingdom", he continued and asked the king if he desired to hear the solution of his questions in a brief or full details of his dream experience. Janaka did not like to have his humiliating dream repeated in presence of a big gathering, hence agreed to receive a brief answer.

Ashtavakra then whispered into the ear of Janaka, "Neither this nor that is real." king Janaka at once became joyful. His confusion was removed.

King Janaka then asked Ashtavakra, "What is real?" Then that young scholar replies, "O King, neither the waking state nor the dream state is real. When you are awake, the world of dreams does not exist and when you dream the world of the senses does not exist. Therefore, neither is real."

"If both the waking and the dream states are unreal, then what is real?" asked the King

"There is a state beyond these two. Discover that. It alone is real" said the sage. If we observe, there is only one thing in common in both dream and waking state. The seer! The one who sees the dream is common. That's the ultimate reality. Our goal is to realize that seer. The nature of him is Sachidananda.

The Seer is the self, who was there here before we born and will be there even after we die. The seer is obscured in us, like that of a hidden sculpture in a marble stone. As Michael Angelo is reported to have said that, every block of marble contained a statue, and the sculptor brought it to light by cutting away the encumbrances by which the " human face divine is concealed." Even so we have to cut away the encumbrances, and remove the obstacles for the expression of the infinite.

Art can awaken powers and kindle the spiritual aspiration. It touches the heart and warms emotions. It is a highway to the human soul. "A thing of beauty is joy forever", Art need not be meant to impress the world but just to transcend its creator. Art is confronting the self, face to face! It helps us surrender to the nature and become one with it. The nature reveals its secrets to him who keeps the door of his heart open always. Vincent Van Gogh painted the stars as spirals, more than a hundred years ago!. The great Indian classical musician Tansen could light up Diyas(oil lamps) with his singing through raag deepak. Artist is a means through whom the soul of the universe expresses. A life without the Art is like a well without the water. Eventually the well will turn into a dustbin. Upanishads are the greatest philosophy written in a poetic way, they feed the intellect with reasoning and also the emotions with insights and aesthetic experiences, only because they were created in the midst of nature and out of direct intuition. Creativity is the very nature of an artist. If that is the case, the god is also an artist. Therefore cultivating art in us is like hosting the god in our very being.

Being an artist, Nolan said "Chase your reality". Vedanta says, In order to chase the reality, you have to be real in first place. So explore that reality in you. When you find the reality in yourself', there will not be any need of chasing the ultimate reality because, reality is only one.

In Vedanta, there are multiple ways to comprehend the reality, either of them can be followed or even the combination of them. Jesus Christ mostly preferred and followed Bhaktiyoga. It is easy to understand the meaning of them and become a half boiled prodigy or Pundit, but it's great if one can cling to them and practice in day to day life.

Love the Truth: Love everything and everyone around you, till the stream of love encircles you with the universe. When there is selfless love towards god or this universe, there will be a feeling of surrendered-ness. You will be the epitome of love. Only the love flows through you, the love of god and the love of truth. Then you will be one with the truth. Just the way an iceberg turns into water, it has water in it or it is water in a different form, color and name. It floats on the water and becomes one with the water.

'Work'-out the Truth: It's a path of action; we need to work with all dedication without any attachment. Doing work with utmost love and having no thought for one's own fame or reward. It is also called as Karmayoga. In Bhagavad-Gita Krishna preaches Arjuna, You have the right to work only but never to its fruits.

'Discipline' the Truth: It's all about self-control and restraint. Maharshi Patanjali has formulated this path of Yoga, it is the king among all four and hence 'Raja Yoga'. It employs the method of self-discipline and practice, for the attainment of truth. It is also known as Ashtanga Yoga (Eight Steps of Yoga), because it is organised in eight steps that are to be followed and achieved sequentially.

Yama (Self-control), Niyama (Discipline), asana (Physical exercises), Pranayama (Breath exercises), Pratyahara (Withdrawal of the senses from external objects), Dharana (Concentration), Dhyana (Meditation), Samadhi (Complete Realisation)

'Know' the Truth: Ask yourself 'Who am I' and keep dropping all other thoughts till you find the answer, for example, if someone asks, who are you ? Ideally you will say your name, say ' I am Jack'. So it's your name, not you! When someone further asks, answer might be 'An engineer or doctor' the profession. If it happens to be an Indian, he will answer I am son of X or Y as he identifies himself with his father. After sometime, the answer might be, I am this! You may say pointing at your own body. So you are the one who is pointing and how can you be the pointed? Then you are not the body. If you are not the body, you must not be something gross or physical. You are being asked certain questions and you are thinking to answer them back. 'You' know that you are thinking! So 'you' are not the mind either. Mind ceases when the thinking stops. 'You' are behind and beyond the mind. You are that which is not! This process of knowing the self through reasoning and intellect is known as Jnanayoga.

There was one of the greatest intellects and philosophers, a Jnanayogi named Adi Shankara in India. He is the force behind complete revamp and rejuvenation of Hinduism. Spiritual history of India had a deep impact by this young monk. He professed Advaita Vedanta and wrote commentaries on Prasthanathrayi. They are considered as the most prodigious and finest works in the history of Vedanta philosophy.

There is an interesting incident in the life of this holy man Shri Shankaracharya. It is said that, when Shankara was a young boy of eight and wandering near River Narmada, seeking to find his guru, he encountered the seer Govinda Bhagavatpada who asked him, "Who are you?" The boy answered with the verses which are known as "Nirvana Shatkam" or 'Athma Shatkam'. Swami Govindapada was amazed by the acumen of the Shankara, who looked like a fresh and sharp sword. Shri. Govindapada accepted Sankara as his disciple the very next moment. The verses are said to be valued to progress in contemplation practices that lead to self-realization. 'Nirvana' is complete equanimity, peace, tranquility, freedom and joy. 'Athma' is the True Self.

Athma Shatkam

manobuddhyahankara cittani naham na ca srotrajihve na ca ghrananetre |
na ca vyoma bhoomirna tejo na vayu cidanandaroopa shivoham
shivoham ||1||

Mind-intellect-thought-ego am I not, neither have I ears, tongue, nor nostrils, nor eyes;
I am not the five great elements; I am Pure Consciousness, Bliss, the Self;
I am Auspiciousness, Auspiciousness alone.

na ca pranasamjno na vai pancavayu na va saptadhatu: na va pancakosa |
na vakpanipadam na copasthapayu cidanandarupa shivoham
shivoham ||2||

The vital-air I am not, Nor have I anything to do with the physiological functions in my body;
Nor am I the seven-fold material that goes into the building up of the body;
Nor am I in any way attached to the five sheaths of my personality;
I have nothing to do with the five organs of action, I am Auspiciousness, Auspiciousness alone.

na me dvesharagau na me lobhamohau mado naiva me naiva matsaryabhava |
na dharmo na cartho na kamo na moksha cidanandarupa shivoham
shivoham ||3||

I have neither likes or dislikes, nor have I covetousness or greed, nor I have any arrogant vanity nor any competition with anyone; Im not even a need for the four main 'purposes of life' I am Auspiciousness, Auspiciousness alone.

> na punyam na papam na saukhyam na dukham na mantro na tirtho na veda na yajna |
> aham bhojanam naiva bhojyam na bhokta cidanandarupa shivoham shivoham ||4||

Sin or merit can never touch me, Joy and sorrow cannot contaminate me; I know no mantra, I have no sacred pilgrimage to make, I know neither scripture, nor have I anything to gain through rituals; I am neither the experiencer (subject), nor the experienced (object), nor the experiencing; I am Auspiciousness, Auspiciousness alone.

> na me mrutyusanka na me jatibeda pita naiva me naiva mata na janma |
> na bandhur na mitram gururnaiva Sishya cidanandarupa shivoham shivoham ||5||

I have no death, nor have I any caste or creed distinction; I have neither father nor mother; why! I am never born! I have no kith or kin, I know no guru, nor am I a disciple; I am Auspiciousness, Auspiciousness alone.

> aaha nirvikalpo nirakara rupo vibhutva ca sarvatra sarvendriya a |
> na casangata naiva muktir na meya cidanandarupa sivoham sivoham ||6||

Thought-free am I, formless my only form, I am the vitality behind all sense organs of everyone; neither have I attachment to anything, nor am I free from everything; I am all-inclusive; I am Auspiciousness, Auspiciousness alone.

Entire Vedanta is encapsulated in these 6 stanzas. Adi Shankara is said to have lived in $8^{th} - 9^{th}$ century, he was an enlightened soul and had this deeper insight about the universe and existence at a small age. Even if we debate and say it's not possible, and consider he wrote this latter part of his life, still its remarkable because he lived for only 32 years on this planet. Shankara was unvanquished and won the hearts of every Indian and traversed extensively in all four directions of the subcontinent to spread his ideas with unparalleled intelligence and wisdom. Whole of India revered him as Jagadguru(guru of universe). His teaching can be summarized in one line as 'Shruti-Yukti-Anubhuthi' . Shruti is Scriptures or the Shastras, Yukti is reasoning and Anubhuti is the experience, the universal experience.

Vedanta was proved to be a panacea. It provides solutions to all problems of the world. If we look at the history, Gauthama Buddha preached Vedanta to fix the issues of the society 2500 years ago. Jagadguru Basavanna, a social reformer of 12th century was influenced by Vedanta and he employed it to eradicate caste-ism and superstitions in the society. At the time of Swami Vivekananda, there was a famine and people were dying with hunger. Vivekananda utilized Vedanta to uplift the poor and to curb poverty. He preached charity and service to the man as service to the god. Mahatma Gandhi exercised it for freedom struggle and succeeded in it. Martin Luther King was in turn inspired from Gandhi and so on. When a principle can solve problems of a nation and the world, where are the problems of an individual. Vedanta elevates an individual to an extra higher realm where he lives like another star in the sky. Personal problems are for the mind and the body, not to the self. Pain is in the mind, you are not responsible for it, Suffering is discretionary, and you can accept it or deny it. You are beyond all of this.

Once you know that you are Sachidananda, you realize that you are here to reveal and know the divinity of your-self. Then what on this earth can bother you, when you are the center of this vast boundless universe. This job, money, lust, relationships, homework, deadline, your skin color or your bodily deficiencies what else?. You are a chunk of manifested divinity, how can you be unholy, how can you be unworthy? Even a blade of grass has utmost significance and proves its existence. Enjoy everything that comes your way, but don't get too much attached to it.

Shri Nolan says, *Chase your reality! Not at the cost of your dreams but as a foundation of your dreams.* The reality is to be chased but not at the cost of dreams. He intends to say, you need not become a monk and go into the forest ignoring the entire world and appreciable creations of man. You need not get into isolation, be in the world, achieve your goals and ambitions. But remember, in that very process of achievement, chase the reality. The love of truth should be the undercurrent and driving force in your endeavors. Nolan's entire life and philosophy is hidden in this one sentence. He chose filmmaking as his profession; He wanted to make a difference to the world by considering reality as the foundation. He tried to chase it in some or the other way in his films. He contemplates on it, reflects on it, attempts to comprehend and helped others as well. Try to find the reality through your worldly dreams. Need not walk up to Himalayas alone; take the entire generation with you; sipping coffee once in a while and winking at the people who approach you. Go gentle into the day light, love the light, live with light and rage if it dusks, don't let your light die. You are the fortunate; you know that night is going to fall, don't let it takeaway the fluoresce of your smile. Smile and Smile with the shining sun, beautifully and eternally.

No matter who you are, what profession you are in, what country you live in, what circumstances you go through, whether you be in a prison or a palace, a beggar or a scion of royal crown, you still can chase the reality because you are the reality! You are that, which is not!

Om Asato Maa Sad-Gamaya |
Tamaso Maa Jyotir-Gamaya |
Mrtyor-Maa Amrtam Gamaya |
Om Shaantih Shaantih Shaantih ||

Om, O Lord, Keep me not in the Unreality, but lead me towards the Reality,
O Lord Keep me not in the Darkness, but lead me towards the Light,
O Lord Keep me not in the Fear of Death, but lead me towards the Immortality
Om, May there be Peace, Peace, Peace

Words of Fame

- He received the Modern Master Award, the highest honor presented by the Santa Barbara International Film Festival.

- He was honored with the first-ever Founder's Award from the Slamdance Film Festival in the year 2014.

- He was selected as the 2015 Class Day speaker at Princeton University.

- Nolan was awarded the Empire Inspiration Award at the 20th Empire Awards in 2015 He received an honorary doctorate in literature (DLit) in 2017

- On 3 May 2017 Nolan received the 2017 FIAF Award before a special 7

Chapter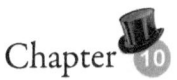

Random thoughts of an unaccomplished mind

There are many ways and forms of expression in writing, sometimes even a three liner can give insights and make us think, and there are examples that, lives are changed by reading a single quote. My life took a different turn after reading a quote, "Give a man a fish, and you feed him for a day. Teach a man to fish, and you feed him for a lifetime" A Navajo proverb. I always thought, I should do something to the people, I should feed them and I should fight for poverty but after certain extent of time, my view got changed, what matters is education and intellectual evolution, that's what helps man for the ages! If you help someone financially it is a social utility and it never helps the beneficiary grow intellectually or psychologically. Gift a book instead of greeting card or a costly chocolate.

Shri Swami Vivekananda said, *"take care about what you think. Words are secondary. Thoughts live; they travel far".* Nothing lasts, after our departure but our thoughts. There have been many kings before and after Gautama Buddha, They had built great mansions and won battles, but never revered and admired by the generations like that done for Buddha. There were many prime ministers and presidents, but none are venerated like MK Gandhi, only the thoughts remain and keep the thinker alive in the minds of people, not the material possessions nor the fame.

A Fistful of Lines:

✦ Only beneficial intoxicant in the world is Spirituality

- All of us are offenders in the past, but what is fortunate is, we are the advocates for our own case and we are the judges. We can always release ourselves from the jail of misery and regrets.

- Whenever you phone call somebody, ask the first question "what you doing?". This way you bring them into the present and help them in their spiritual evolution!!

- If Buddha was lived a king, he wouldn't have been revered like now, everyone should try to find truth apart from materialistic goals.

- Death is like tiger Richard Parker in the film 'Life Of Pie', it keeps you alive, if you are awake, attentive and keep a watch on it. It kills you, if you ignore it

- If your relationship is independent and above the layers of wealth, physical beauty, family, and behavior, you won't breakup, no matter what.

- The true artist is the truth in him.

- Mind compares, but you should discriminate! Intuition is the mother of reasoning, the reasoning gives you answers, and Intuition gives you truth

- Why are we living? Because we are sborn! Why are we born? Because we have to live!.

- If you have the time to give time some time, there won't be a time that you will curse the time.

- A day will come when the sun shines for you in midnight! And you will fail to recall the nature of darkness, because you would forget of how to remember.

- Someone said, don't become a philosopher until you become rich, i say rich men can't become philosophers, because how can they win over their mind, when they are already lost to money! Wise earn money for the freedom; stupid earns to become a better slave!

- If you want to be happy, you should learn to be lazy sometimes, should break the rules and daily schedule, after all heroes are meant to break rules.

- There is a difference between robot and man with mobile phone! Robot will alarm when its battery is low and hungry,

- The benefit of reading is you will gain knowledge; and of writing is you will process that into wisdom!

- Its great to have the habit of writing Diary, writing makes you face yourself and accept yourself as what you are and remove all the masks of Hypocrisy.

- Dont think yourself great when you give away your money or possessions, there are people who gave themselves.

- Dont wear the golden shoes called success too early, you might lag behind, because metallic shoes hurt.

- Possessiveness is not love and the love without possessiveness is not love too.

- I always thought there is a philosopher in me! But now i realized that there is an ordinary man in a philosopher!

- It's better to have a girlfriend than to drink alcohol.

- There is nothing wrong to be a mediocre, but forcing creativity will end up being more mediocre.

- It's better to encourage teenagers to go for a date, than sending them to communal outfits and all that nonsense.

- Intuition is the language of god!, The more intuitive you are, the more closer you are with the god.

- If you think, what you said last year is absolute nonsense; it shows that you are growing up.

- The beauty of Vedanta is, It preaches god as a thought and thought as god. No conflict but a commune.

- If you can draw a tree, exactly the way it is, then i will prefer the original one!

- If you become an astronaut you can go to mars, If you become a yogi, you can cross the galaxies.

- I stopped seeking since the time i met you, i see myself in you, and you are my mirror.

- There were no examples of mass enlightenment, it's just the individual.

- If you are always in a herd, your nature will be of sheep.

- Everyone on this earth is alone! They just create some people around as their subjective world and convince themselves that they are happy. And not afraid of anything! Just imagine if you are alone in this entire universe.

- There is no point in dying for some cause, when we can live for it. It's wise to live long and fulfill it, than to die in an excitement/aggression.

- When you open a pomegranate, you see the glory of creator, arrangement of the seeds, the crystal pearl like pattern, the shiny color and full of life, but all that came from the soil, how you can be still an atheist.

- Learning is quite easier than unlearning the things, its mandatory to learn to unlearn.

- There is always something to learn, because what we learn always is just something.

- Disaster of man is, being learned he limits himself to a religion, a country, a faith, a race when he has the whole universe for him.

- Art can be used for intellectual evolution of man, not just the mere imitation of nature.

- There is always something to do, even for god! What we do should reach to an extent where it diminishes the time.

- When i loved deep down myself, sometimes i was suspicious that i am being selfish and self-obsessed, but now i realized, it was my preparation to love you deep down to the very core of you.

- When you watch more movies, you predict next scene. When you read more books, you predict next paragraph, when you experience life closely, you predict future, but prediction need not be true always.

- Nightingales sing, flowers bloom, tigers roar, none of them are levied tax by the government. Farmers and Artists are like that for a nation; they should be exempted from tax or should be given concession.

- Few are ready to believe that Jesus Christ was born for a virgin, but not the fact that meditation in long run, leads to enlightenment and immortality.

- Knowing that you are insane is the first step to become sane!

- If you don't leave your past, your present will leave you

- Before trying to understand possibly existing higher dimensions, did we really understand how to escape the known dimensions of time and space?

- Man becomes more defensive when he lies more, and gradually it leads to disintegration of the self and creates a whirl of chaos in mind. This will disable capability of mind to evolve. This is the reason, religions teach morals.

- Silence heals, because it won't create further conflicts, at least in the long run, it heals.

- Thinking is forcing the mind to be on one thought, when the act of forcefulness is removed, it becomes meditation.

- Films that make you feel are one kind, films that make you think are superior, but films that make you experience are the ultimate because they include former two as well.

- When I travel in airplane or the subway train, I feel my 'self' is constant. In both cases I cover the time and space, hence the 'Self' is out of these realms.

- Sometimes it's the stone in shoe that causes trouble, which we misinterpret as the stony path.

- When you are in the crowd, It's better to behave like a sheep,

- When you read about a hypocrite character you will know the hypocrisy in you, when you read about a killer you realize your criminal nature, reading is the process of cleansing the dust on the mirror of self.

- If you feel like having a beer, watch a Martin Scorsese's film; If you want to be an innocent child again watch a Spielberg movie. If you feel like reading a suspense thriller, watch a Hitchcock's movie. And if you want some enlightenment, watch a Nolan's movie.

- Everyone is a freedom fighter during their teenage and everyone is a ruler during their parenthood. Celebration of Independence day is meaningful!

- You can allow your parents to choose you partner, If you allow them to buy undergarments for you.

- Creativity is an inherent nature of man. It is crippled by the social conditioning and destroyed by so called education.

- All religions promise you heaven or the hell. Vedanta will not let you die in first place.

- The society prepares you for a race. Whether to run an infinite rat race or climb the hill of wisdom like a lonely wolf is left to your conscience.

- Truth of love can only be experienced when there is a love of truth.

- Juveniles go after money, sex and fame. Adults go after knowledge, Legends lead a Yogic Life.

- Let everyone try to become something, you just BE that something.

- When 'HE', goes after the 'ART', It completes his 'HEART'.

- Being moral may not take you to heaven after the death, but it gives you a glimpse of it when you are alive.

- Enlightenment and Orgasm are both personal affairs. Yet, both are treated poles apart by man.

- Former is a fantasized fact and latter the factual fantasy. One shouldn't be burdened by either of them, but both are worth giving a try

Once Upon a time in my mind

Limbo

I am aware of this place, but not like the way it is now.
There used to be a fair here, full of crowd and commotion.
Now, it's all void and a wide space with no ends.
It's full of emptiness.
I see someone standing tall from far away.
With a sense respite and curiosity, I headed towards him.
Every step that i moved closer, he got dwindled.
When i reached him and tried to confront, I ceased to exist!.
What about him?

You need Courage to gain courage!:

It's very interesting to know, how the paradox of Vedanta works. Sometimes it is as rigid as the Card Paradox but of a different nature. Say for example, i want to be bold and do to something. I need courage for that. In order to gain courage, i follow some strange practice. I style my hair like that of a Samurai. Because I am inspired by a samurai culture of Japan, their self-discipline, dedication, grace, compassion and most of all, their courage is really worth admiring. So in order to style my hair like a Samurai, i need courage, the courage to face stereotypical society. Therefore I need courage to gain courage. Bruce Wayne needs courage to go into the bat cave and win over his fear to become courageous. Only courage can lead you to the courage. Same way In Vedanta, In order to achieve the concentration, we need to concentrate. The watcher and the watched, knower and the known, experiencer and the experienced are the same.

✦ Monkey and Evolution :

Once we were sitting for lunch on a fine afternoon, my colleague uttered something strange but with lot of proud and pomp. She said "A monkey stops by our balcony every day, we feed him always. We feed him only dry-fruits and he refuses to accept anything else". She was expecting appreciation from us for the great cause being done by her family. I replied "This is utter nonsense. You are snatching the right of monkey to search for the food; its intellectual evolution will be crippled by your act. If you feed dry-fruits to it, it will settle for this very life of a monkey, it never wishes to become a man. The evolution stops, when the struggle ends". I just said it to make her think in another angle, she never dared to toss such nonsensical discussion again.

✦ Old wine in new bottle:

It's about the wine that tastes a little bitter initially but the sweetest by the time we finish it, not the European wine but Asian, in fact very old. We already know that we can practice Vedanta in our day to day life, just having the thought that 'I' am not the body and 'I' am not the mind. All the pains or sufferings arise in either of them, so 'I' need not or doesn't bothered or disturbed. We are practicing it in the midst of most happening, colorful and busiest world around. We have family and kids. No matter how much we convince ourselves that we are not the mind, the world will drag down and mind supports it. We know theoretically what to be done but we are unable to practice it and may 'become an old man, filled with regret, waiting to die?' So, do you want to take a leap of faith?' Saito said in Inception. Dom Cob took the leap of faith, so it is worth a try isn't it?

We are here to enjoy this world, our wealth, power, family, spouse, children, foreign trips etc. Having all this around, we may not achieve fruitful results in terms of spirituality, so ancient Indians had devised a method, the sweet wine that we are talking about. It is nothing but Ashrama system, in which life is devided into 4 stages namely Brahmacharya (Student: Till the age 24), Grihastha (Householder: 24 to 48), Vanaprastha (Retired life:48 to 72), Sanyasa (Renounced life:72+ or anytime). This method ensures that man will experience all the essence of human life and will not miss anything. As it may not be possible for us to follow these stages strictly, we can try the last two, when we feel fulfilled with the family life. Vanaprastha is the phase of transition i.e handing over the wealth and responsibilities to the next successor generations and to be in an advisory role. It's to detach from the desires of Kama(pleasure) and Artha(wealth, ambitions) and gradually emphasizing on Moksha(Spiritual Liberation). In the last phase of 'sanyasa', one can go and lead a monastic life with complete renunciation. An example for the life lived in this system is of an ancient Indian King Chandragupta Mourya(about 298BC-320CE). He lived the fullest of life, he was an orphan raised under the tutelage of Chanakya, builds the biggest empire in the history of Indian subcontinent and wins over all the contemporary kings, marries a most beautiful queen, and at last renounces everything, becomes an ascetic and then finally leaves the body after nirvana(enlightenment). What a tremendous approach for life.

In the modern world, retirement age from the work is 60 years. At least after this, one can practice spiritual life and enjoy his/her own company and try to understand the nature of existence and life. However except a class of people, what we see is, exactly the opposite. Many people even at the older age seek relationships and possess sexual desires. It is evident that after retirement many Europeans fly to East Asian countries to fulfill their thirst of worldly pleasures. How long should it happen? Many modern Indians at this age are still hunger for wealth, relationships and rest of the world also is no different. It may seem that, we will be afraid of loneliness or the pain of leaving. There is nothing to leave off but to release the attachments gradually and attempt to establish a commune with the god. It's always better to release off consciously when alive than to unconsciously and forcefully by death. No one on earth is spared from birth and death, hence all have to try to understand the nature of it at least once in life time. So in order to taste and experience the amrita(elixir), we should be ready to drink this old wine of retired life and renunciation.

✦ Yogi of Yogis:

Lord Krishna is the epitome of yogic life. He has highest prominence and presence throughout the story of Mahabharata, but nowhere you see him crying, broken out, confused, depressed, dejected or with any ill motives like other characters. He is involved in everything, war and peace, pleasure and pain but not attached to anything. He is there but not really! He is the embodiment of the principle of SthithaPrajna. Krishna achieved the state of a Yogi, being in the midst of the Samsara. Every human being can live like Krishna, this is the greatest lesson one can learn from the epic Mahabharata. Everyone has the potential to be a yogi.

Vedanta in a Nutshell:

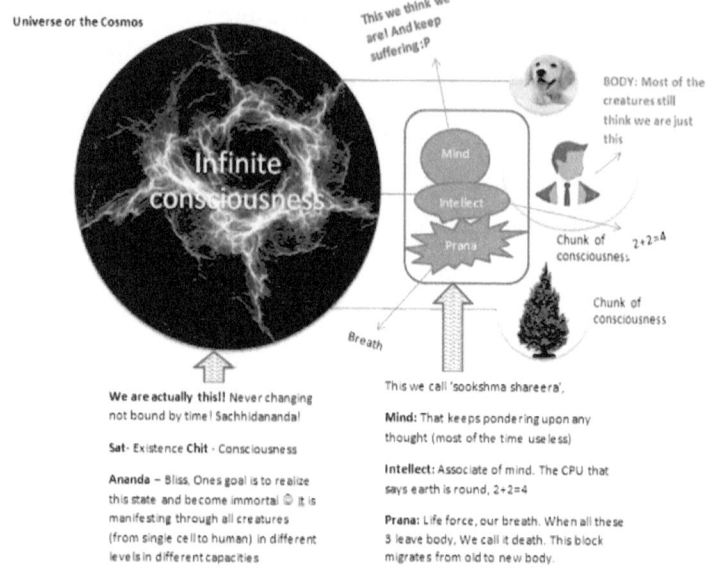

Figure 10.2 Vedanta

Words of Fame

- He was honored with the first-ever Founder's Award from the Slamdance Film Festival in the year 2014.
- He was selected as the 2015 Class Day speaker at Princeton University.
- He received an honorary doctorate in literature (DLit) in 2017
- On 3 May 2017 Nolan received the 2017 FIAF Award before a special 70 mm screening of Interstellar at the Samuel Goldwyn Theater in Beverly Hills.
- He was honored with a handprint and footprint ceremony on July 7, 2012 at Grauman's Chinese Theater in Los Angeles, becoming the youngest director ever.
- He received best director academy award nomination for the film 'Dunkirk'.

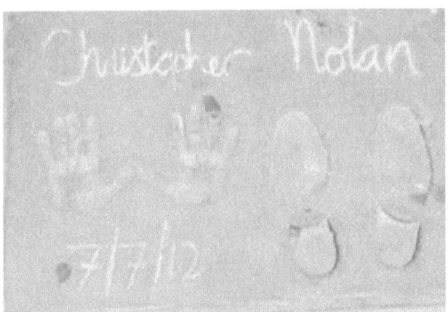

Figure 10.2 Nolan's hand and shoeprints in front of the Grauman's Chinese Theatre in Hollywood

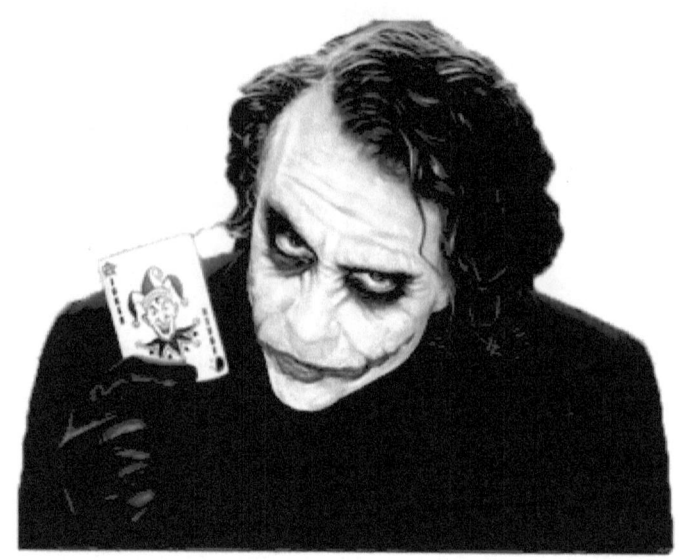

Why so serious?

Did you read closely? "Yogi in Suits" Is just a symbol, and everybody can be a Yogi!

It's time to close the book, forget all that you read, Lets watch over the mind, what's happening?

You still have a thought, a thought of watching over the mind itself. No, remove that as well. Do it again! No don't do it, doing again is forcing, so don't force. Just be.

"The dust of the dead words cling to thee, wash thy soul with silence."
- Tagore

www.ingramcontent.com/pod-product-compliance
Lightning Source LLC
Chambersburg PA
CBHW020655220526
45464CB00001B/446